Success Stories

"Alan, what you do for people is very special. You rapidly taught me how to minimize the negatives in my mind. In addition you taught me how to acquire a positive yet practical perspective on life. This has resulted in me doing so much better, both at work and in my social life."

B.L.

"No more restless nights. Alan, thanks to your ability and dedication I am now sleeping well."

S.P.

"My physician referred me to Alan to reduce my anxiety. A few sessions later I was amazed at my ability to remain calm and free of anxiety, even in difficult situations."

N.R.

"For years I was trampled on by others. Alan's techniques helped me get my voice back."

K.N.

"Alan is gifted. He caringly helped me overcome my issues and achieve the important goals in my life."

G.B.

"Every morning I wake up feeling great. My sales are up. The techniques are working and I now know how to "step" into the Winning Zone."

D.M.

"The life coaching tools and techniques I learned from Alan were instrumental in my ability to overcome test anxiety and pass my master's degree exam. I don't think I could have passed without them."

R.W.

i

A GUIDE TO HAPPINESS

Tips, tools and techniques
for dealing with life's
issues and for increasing
motivation

Alan Shein

Printed in the United States of America

ISBN 978-0-9980017-0-8

The entire contents of this book are for educational and self-improvement
purposes only, and are not intended in any way to be a replacement for the
diagnosis or treatment of any psychiatric, psychological or medical ailment. If
you believe you may have a condition visit a medical professional, and do not
attempt any of the techniques, ideas, or suggestions in this book without his
or her consent. The visualizations found in this book are not to be practiced
by anyone who suffers from schizophrenia or epilepsy. No warranties or
guarantees are expressed or implied by the author or publisher's choice to
include any of the content of this book. The author, publisher and all parties
involved in the distribution of this book shall not be liable for any personal
injury, financial loss, or any other commercial or consequential damages
resulting from its use. Please be advised that the entire contents of this book
are solely the opinion of the author.

CAUTION: Do not practice the techniques calling for you to close your eyes
while driving or operating any form of transport, whilst moving about, when
operating or being in the proximity of machinery, or whenever alertness is
needed.

This book is available at special quantity pricing to corporations, professional
associations and for fundraising and educational purposes. For further
information send an email to sales@WestStarPublishing.com

Illustration concepts by Alan Shein
Illustrations by Chris Davis
Book design by Chris Davis
Author photography by Elsa Flores

**This book is dedicated to
the memory of my father, David Shein.**

Along his road through life,
he had more than his share of difficulties and challenges,
but his strength of character,
his willingness to improve his skills and knowledge,
and his resolute perseverance overcame them.

He believed that, with due effort and desire,
anything within the bounds of practicality
could be attained or overcome.
Whenever doubt or hesitation step into my thoughts,
I am reminded of his words and advice to me:
"Where there is a will there is a way."

These words, when needed, help drive and steer me
in the direction of doing and achieving.
If you see value and wisdom in these words
and feel they would be of use to you,
then take them and place them in your tool-box
and use them whenever you could do
with an extra helping nudge forward.

Foreword

by Dr. David Bortz

For those wanting a sensible, effective and efficient approach to dealing with life's stressors, this is a helpful book that gets to the heart of helping to resolve many of life's everyday issues.

Light, refreshing and on target, the content in each chapter comes across with clarity and a feeling of genuine care for the reader. For quick and easy reference the author has placed each of the many categories addressed into its own self-contained chapter.

Many chapters have illustrations. The combination of the author's writings and the visuals he conceptualized and directed is a welcome element to the self-improvement and motivation category; furthermore it is bound to enhance the reading experience and effectiveness of this book.

As a physician, I find that the majority of my patients' problems are caused or aggravated by anxiety and related disorders. I see this book helping to speed up their progress in dealing with these issues.

People today are often pressed for time and want to make progress as fast as possible — they want easy-to-apply techniques and they want them now!

Alan's direct, easy to follow tools and techniques can quickly be put into practice. I have recommended him to my patients for many years to work through their anxieties, stress, diminished self-confidence, phobias, habits and sleeping difficulties.

I have to believe that this book will also contribute to decreasing stress in the workplace leading to higher productivity and calmer spaces.

Finally, I recommend that medical practitioners and allied health professionals have a copy of this book, not just to suggest to patients, but to help themselves in dealing with the stress of running a practice.

Dr. David Bortz
M.D., F.A.C.P.
Associate Professor Of Medicine
University Of California, San Diego

Table of Contents

How to Use This Book

My Dear Readers,

This is a how-to book. In the following pages, you will find many of the tips, tools and techniques that, over the years, have proven successful for my clients. These ideas and exercises can help you make important changes in your life, increase your levels of happiness, relaxation and tranquility, and help you set and achieve goals.

To get the most out of this book, I suggest that you have a quick read of the first five chapters and then go directly to the specific chapter or chapters that interest you. From there you will begin to work through the issues and subjects that are most relevant to you right now. If you find new issues arise down the road, revisit this book and turn to the relevant chapters.

Because we live in a rush-rush, pressure-filled world, I'm sure it would please you to know that the tools and techniques in this book take very little time to do, and require no special equipment.

I invite you to view this success-oriented book as a partnership between you and me. My contribution to the partnership is sharing the techniques which I have successfully taught my clients over the years. Your contribution to this partnership is to devote just minutes out of your day to practice the techniques related to attaining your goal. Just like wanting to attain anything worthwhile, the more you practice, the more positive will be the outcome. If you choose to uphold this partnership you will likely begin experiencing the benefits the book describes and simultaneously you will begin developing a stronger and more positive foundation for your future.

It took you time, probably years, to form the thought patterns and habits that you are now finding troublesome. Be assured that even a slight move in a positive direction will bring you greater peace and happiness and a feeling of accomplishment.

Take this book with you wherever you go. Keep it close. It will be a useful tool to have along your path of life.

Alan Shein

Note: Some chapters are interrelated and to allow for a more effective reading experience may contain some overlap. Just as playing a piano takes repetitive practice, any overlap will also provide useful repetition which in and of itself is therapeutic and speeds the pathway to success.

Chapter 1

The Positive Effects Of Tranquility

"The more tranquil a man becomes, the greater is his success, his influence, his power for good. Calmness of mind is one of the beautiful jewels of wisdom."   James Allen

Sometimes, life throws curve balls and challenges at us. However, if you catch them with tranquility, you are more likely to respond in a calm, clear and logical way. A state of tranquility will keep you in control and in the present.

When in a tranquil and relaxed state, there is far less tendency to over-react or say something that you will later regret. Equally important, when in this frame of mind, you are being kind to your body. This happens because tranquility causes a reduction of the stress hormone, cortisol, from flooding into your body and harming your immune system.

Feeling tranquil and relaxed frees you to enjoy increased well-being and optimism. This state also tends to reduce physical stress and tension which can cause all sorts of mental and physical problems.

Practice the techniques offered in this book and you will be on your way to experiencing a life filled with a heightened sense of peace and serenity. When those curve balls come out of nowhere, you will be better prepared to catch them.

Tranquility makes for an easier day.

Chapter 2

The Mind-Body Connection

"If there were no mind-body connection, the neck would be looking for a job." The Author

The mind-body connection is widely acknowledged by medical professionals as playing a vitally important role in our daily lives.

Because of the existence of the mind-body connection, the mind has an effect on the body and the body has an effect on the mind. It is widely acknowledged by medical professionals that our perceptions, beliefs, feelings and attitudes can both positively and negatively affect the physiology and overall working of our bodies. For example, stressful, anxious or fearful thoughts can turn into physical issues in our bodies in the form of sweating, rapid heartbeat, high blood pressure, muscular tension, skin breakouts, knots in the stomach, appetite changes, dizziness and other symptoms.

Conversely, and also because of the mind-body connection, when we recall a time when we were joyful or calm, our bodies tend to feel calmer and more relaxed.

Proof of the existence of the mind-body connection is found in the following demonstration:

> *Imagine putting a slice of a juicy orange or lemon in your mouth and biting into it. Imagine the scented aroma of the fruit. As you*

take one refreshing bite after another, sense or imagine the tasty juices spraying into every corner of your mouth and onto each and every taste bud on your tongue. Have a few more bites and continue tasting the delicious juices.

You will notice that salivation or mouthwatering has occurred, yet there was no orange or lemon. It was just the thought of the tasty fruit that caused the salivary glands to produce the saliva. The messages from the mind were able to reach the salivary glands because of the existence of the mind-body connection.

The following chapter on guided imagery and visualization illustrates how the potential of your mind and the understanding of the mind-body connection can help you in your daily life.

Chapter 3

Visualization and Guided Imagery

"Visualize this thing that you want, see it, feel it, believe in it. Make your mental blueprint, and begin to build."

Robert Collier

Visualization is increasingly used to enhance quality of life, to achieve specific goals, and to improve outcomes in healthcare settings. It has been used as a therapeutic technique as far back as the ancient civilizations of Greece, Rome, India, Egypt, and China.

Visualization is a gentle but powerful technique that uses your creative imagination and the power of your subconscious mind to help you resolve issues and increase your potential to succeed. You've heard of athletes who, before a race, "see" themselves striding toward the finishing line. Monitoring equipment has shown that when these athletes visualize or imagine themselves performing at their peak level, their muscles twitch and the associated neural pathways fire as if they were actually running the race. When they go onto the track, they have run the race so often in their minds that their bodies follow the course already set by the mind. Accomplished speakers prepare themselves for their presentations by "seeing and hearing" their audiences responding enthusiastically to their speeches. Another example of visualization could be you "seeing" yourself being tranquil and composed in difficult circumstances. **Albert Einstein recognized the power of the imagination and visualization—he stated that "what you see in your imagination is the preview of what is to be."**

Visualization and guided imagery are associated with the mind-body connection, which is described in the previous chapter.

Some of the applications of visualization:
Among visualization's many applications, it can be used to help reduce stress and blood pressure, overcome anxiety and fears, reduce weight, manage pain, and accelerate healing. It allows you to rapidly achieve a relaxed state by using your mind or imagination to transport you to a peaceful place, like a beach or a garden. When practiced regularly, this activity leads to a reduction in everyday stress levels and boosts feelings of well-being, calm, and tranquility. Visualizing is frequently used by aspiring and professional business people to increase their performance and confidence.

In healthcare settings, visualization is also referred to as guided imagery. The difference between the two is that visualization is usually done alone, whereas a guided imagery session is conducted by a person trained in guided imagery techniques. Because of its positive healing and calming effects, visualization or guided imagery is increasingly endorsed and used by leading hospitals across the country including: Stanford Hospital (CA), The Cleveland Clinic (OH), Beth Israel Medical Center (NY), and Duke University Health System (NC). As seen on the TV news magazine show "60 Minutes," military hospitals are also teaching physically and emotionally wounded soldiers how to improve their situations with visualizations.

Fortunately, visualization is easy to learn. Like anything else, your skill will improve with practice. Don't force the visualization process, just relax and let it happen. Persevere, even skeptics become rather good at it!

More About Visualizing

Visualizing is the act of creating specific mental pictures or images of yourself achieving your goals or making your desired improvements. Unlike daydreaming where the mind tends to wander, visualizations done for a purpose are specific, focused and have a pre-determined direction.

Using advanced imaging equipment called P.E.T. scanners (Positron Emission Tomography), scientists have proven that the same parts of the brain are activated when people are on site seeing and experiencing something as when they are many miles away just visualizing or imagining that same thing. Examples of these include visualizing a tropical island sunset or a calm lake surrounded by gently rolling hills. Again, a P.E.T. scan will prove that the same area of the brain is activated, whether you were actually there, on the island or by the lake or just visualizing the scenes. This proves that the subconscious mind cannot tell the difference between what is real and what is imagined. This is part of the reason why visualization is such a successful tool.

To those who say visualizing is a challenge, I invite you to close your eyes and take me on a quick descriptive tour of your home, or describe the physical features of someone you know. You can easily do this. As you progress, visualizing will become easier to do. If visualizing is still a challenge, then "just imagine" what the visual would be. If visualizing is still difficult, shift your focus to what you can hear, feel, taste or smell about the scene. Think of a piece of music, or the feel of an ocean breeze against your skin, a favorite food or a familiar scent.

Visualizations can be strengthened by adding in one or more of the four other senses: hearing, feeling, taste and smell.

Whether you are thinking of a real or made-up place or situation, "See what you see there. Hear what you hear there. Feel what you feel there. Smell what you smell there. Taste what you taste there."

The following is an example of how to do a visualization routine. Use these steps as a guide when doing the other visualization techniques mentioned further in this book.

Positive Visualization

To visualize an improved or more successful you:

1. First read through all five steps without doing the actions.

2. Close your eyes. Picture yourself looking successful, bright and happy.

3. Add whatever special effects that make the picture even more compelling for you. Could be sounds, physical feelings, taste and smell.

4. Increase the picture's size, make the colors stronger and brighter and if you wish frame it and shine spotlights onto it.

5. Think of or imagine how improvement or success feels to you. Now let that feeling soak into you. Imagine it going into every cell in your body. Feel the feeling throughout your whole body, from the top of your head all the way down to the tips of your toes.

6. When you are suitably infused with the feeling of achievement and success, open your eyes and then hold onto the feeling throughout your day. If the feeling fades, repeat the sequence.

Visualization excites and unleashes the power of the subconscious mind to motivate and support your desire to succeed. It also helps you notice and recognize opportunities for you to pursue. Visualization provides the advantage of allowing you to pre-experience the feeling and sight of the accomplishment of your goal. This pre-experience makes the goal's ultimate accomplishment even more desirable and more worth the effort of achieving it. Visualizing can help you to improve or succeed, but in the same way as an athlete trains for an event, a student studies for a test, or a business person puts in the effort toward reaching targets, so you must also put in the appropriate work effort.

Note: Before visualizing or imagining yourself succeeding at a project or reaching a goal, make sure that project or goal is believable, realistic and attainable. If a person has never taken a flying lesson, it is neither believable, realistic, nor attainable, that by next week he or she will be piloting a passenger jet.

With practice, visualizations or imagining become more enhanced and easier to do. Visualize daily, even for just a few minutes. Short, frequent sessions are more effective than long, irregular sessions. Repetition is vitally important. The more clearly you visualize, the faster your mind and body will respond.

Some people prefer to visualize a movie rather than a picture. They both work.

If the achievement of a particular goal seems to large to visualize all at once, break it down into steps and visualize yourself working on and completing one step at a time. Continue in this way until the entire goal is accomplished.

Chapter 4

Thoughts and Feelings

"All that we are is the result of what we have thought. The mind is everything. What we think, we become."

Buddha

See your thoughts as the grand originator, the place where everything starts. Your thoughts are the ignition point that set in motion the dynamic events that influence and ultimately shape your life.

Thoughts------>Feelings------->Actions------>Outcomes

Our thoughts directly and profoundly affect our feelings and emotions. Positive and constructive thoughts lead to positive feelings, which lead to positive actions, which then lead to positive outcomes.

Negative thoughts lead to negative outcomes.

Feelings are often experienced physically. For some, the physical symptom may be a rapid heartbeat, or tightness in the stomach. Others may tremble.

Unpleasant thoughts cause unpleasant feelings—you can interrupt or stop the sequence by questioning the validity of each thought.

Bear strongly in mind that negative thoughts are often not based on fact and are sometimes exaggerated. Just as you don't believe everything you hear or read, don't believe all your thoughts!

Your thoughts determine the directions you take: Thinking the appropriate thoughts is of major importance. This is because we move in the direction of our most dominant thoughts—Think that you can succeed and you increase your chances of succeeding. Think that you can't…well, we all know how that ends.

Thoughts have a powerful influence on our minds and bodies. We discussed in the last chapter that visualizing or imagining a peaceful scene helps our thoughts become calmer. This same process plays a part in sending biochemical messengers to our bodies causing them to also feel calmer. Anxious imaginings do the opposite—they make us feel worried and fearful, mentally and physically.

The following study is an example of how parts of the brain can change physically according to how they are "exercised." Reading on you will see how our repeated thoughts on a particular subject also cause physical change within the brain.

Research studies were carried out by The University College London (UK) on the brains of dozens of trainee cab drivers. To become a licensed London cab driver, one must first pass a difficult test known as "The Knowledge." Studying for this test involves memorizing hundreds of journeys and street names to equip the cab driver with the ability to navigate the quickest routes, depending on current traffic conditions, around this busy, complex city.

For the study, the trainees had MRI brain scans before and after they started studying for "The Knowledge" test. The "after" scans clearly showed that the brain parts linked to memorizing for the test had adapted to their new task by altering their structure and shape.

The research team stated that their findings proved that the brain, when exercised (in this case: studying for the test), has an amazing ability to change. Neuroplasticity is the scientific term for the ability of the brain to alter it structure and shape. With the appropriate exercising, the brain will facilitate the development of the "thought carrying" neural pathways, which, with further exercising will strengthen and change from being narrow tracks to becoming fast and efficient neural highways. This "rewiring" of the brain can occur reasonably quickly leading to beneficial change in habits and increased task performance.

Similarly, if we have consistent positive thoughts about succeeding, the development of "positive" neural pathways associated with increased success will strengthen, leading to positive feelings, success-directed positive actions, and successful outcomes. Negative thoughts produce the opposite effect. *(See diagram on facing page).*

In the same way, the more often the brain experiences a calm and relaxed state, the more the parts of the brain associated with calm and tranquility will increase in prominence, and the brain parts associated with anxiety will decrease in prominence.

Increased happiness is developed in the same way. When our thoughts are more often of a happy nature, the negative or "sad" neural pathways decrease in size and the positive, or "happy" neural pathways increase in size. The increase in path size makes it quicker and easier for us to experience a happier mindset.

THE CREATION AND DEVELOPMENT OF NEURAL PATHWAYS IN THE BRAIN

NEGATIVE PATHWAY

"I don't think I can succeed."

The negative neural pathway begins to develop.

"I really don't think I can succeed."

Repetitive negative thoughts cause the negative neural pathway to strengthen resulting in the negative habit growing stronger.

POSITIVE PATHWAY

"I think I can succeed."

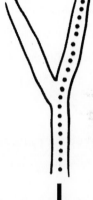

The positive neural pathway begins to develop.

"I can succeed and I will work hard at it."

Repetitive positive thoughts cause the positive neural pathway to strengthen, increasing the buildup of the positive habit.

Chapter 5

The Three Words To Avoid

"Good words are worth much and cost little."

Rudyard Kipling

In addition to negative thoughts leading to negative outcomes, the use of certain words tend to do the same. In order to make the changes you want for yourself and to achieve your goals, it is best to avoid speaking and thinking these three words: TRY, HOPE and SHOULD.

TRY is a set up for failure.

* "I'll try to make the changes to be more productive at work."

  Try shows no real commitment to change or achievement. To achieve success, **replace** the word "try" with a proactive word like "do" or "will." These are "result-getting words" which imply commitment and action.

HOPE is not proactive.

* "I hope the phone at my new business starts ringing soon. Hopefully lots of orders will come through."

  Hope by itself never brings change or success. Success takes effort and never happens because you "hope" it will.

SHOULD is destructive and limiting.

* "I should do exactly what my friends expect of me."

- "I should just accept whatever is handed or said to me."
- "I should never take even the smallest risk."

The word "should" places limits on your actions. These restrictions can lead to guilt, shame, lowered self-esteem, and self-condemnation. Eliminating the "should" contributes to placing you firmly in the driver's seat and back in control of your life.

TRY, HOPE and SHOULD are too negative and limiting to keep in your vocabulary — discard them!

Visualize or imagine all of your "tries, hopes and shoulds" burning in a roaring fire. Feel and sense your growing empowerment and freedom as you watch those limiting words and thoughts go up in flames and disappear. After you have burned them in the bonfire, be on the lookout to see if you ever use any of these three words or thoughts again. If you notice yourself thinking or saying those three words, go to the bonfire and throw them in again and then correct yourself.

Chapter 6

Less Stress

"There is more to life than increasing speed."

Mohandas Gandhi

Many of the people sitting in a doctor's waiting room are there because of a stress-related issue. Stress is a major contributor to absenteeism and lower productivity both in the workplace and in school.

Some of the symptoms and results of stress:

- General aches and pains
- High blood pressure
- Skin conditions
- Insomnia
- Change in appetite
- Decreased work productivity
- Consistent worrying
- Knots in the stomach
- Decreased enjoyment
- Ignoring responsibilities
- Focusing on the negative
- Catastrophic thinking

Visit your doctor to discuss your symptoms and your stress in general. In addition, you can start the healing process by simply asking yourself this VITAL question: **"What is going on in my life right now?"**

Answer this question by writing down the events or circumstances that are currently causing you stress, and then examine them one by one — where possible, take the appropriate action to reduce or eliminate whatever is causing the stress.

Life events such as breakups, relocating, the loss of someone close, job loss, upcoming academic tests, and so many other events and issues are all causes of stress. Each stressor must be resolved as much as is possible and as soon as is possible to prevent any increase in stress levels.

Until the cause of the stress is acknowledged and resolved, the symptoms of the stress are very likely to keep showing up.

It is also useful to accept the fact that at times it is not the actual "things" out there that cause the stress, but rather, how we perceive those things and how we react to them. For example, while some people become stressed out by the sight of spiders or by the thought of an upcoming event, other people perceive those things as non-threatening and are not at all stressed by them. See Chapter 18 – How to Decide What is Really Important and Chapter 44 - Better Perceptions–Better Life.

Declutterize to Optimize

If there was less clutter, chaos and confusion in our personal lives, we would have less stress. We tend to overlook, even ignore, the fact that living in clutter contributes to bringing on stress. In a cluttered space, we can't readily locate our possessions. Have you ever lost your keys, or failed to pay a bill on time because it was hidden under a pile somewhere? How do you feel when this happens? In these situations, your feeling of being in control diminishes, which in itself produces stress. If you can't locate a bill, you are confronted with the next stressful thought of a late fee and possible damage to your credit ratings. The stress caused by this one preventable situation continues to grow and grow. In addition to all this avoidable stress production, there is a huge amount of time wasted by searching for lost items. **Next thing, negative self-talk and recriminations about how disorganized and inefficient we are kick in, dragging us down into a spiral of destructive, stress-producing thoughts**.

One of the solutions to reducing stress is by declutterizing—getting rid of the clutter in your life. Start by declutterizing one shelf, drawer, or small area at a time and then move on to bigger areas and spaces.

More Mess - More Stress

Less Mess - Less Stress

Make a list of the aspects in your life, including your work, home, and social life, which could be improved if there were less clutter and complications attached to them. Write down how you will declutterize and simplify them. I would confidently say that your stress levels related to these and other areas in your life will likely decrease once you have declutterized them and gotten rid of the excess baggage.

Experience a benefit of declutterizing:

, How do you feel when looking at a cluttered surface in your home or office?

Declutterize it, and look again. How do you feel now?

Declutterize one surface or space at a time until the entire area is as it is meant to be.

Since the causes of stress cover such a wide field, take a quick glance at the table of contents and go directly to those chapters that would be helpful to you. My clients have found these same techniques and tools, as detailed in these chapters, to be extremely effective in helping with their various stress issues and now I would like to share them with you.

It is better to deal with stress as a survivor than as a victim.

Chapter 7

Quick and Easy Relaxation Techniques

"Tension is who you think you should be. Relaxation is who you are."   *Chinese Proverb*

The following four techniques promote a state of calm and relaxation.

18-Second Relaxation Technique

1. Sit comfortably

2. Close your eyes

3. Inhale through your nose for a count of 5

4. Hold your breath for a count of 6

5. Exhale slowly through your mouth for a count of 7

6. While exhaling, you might want to say or think a word that brings tranquility to you. Such a word might be "peace" or "calm".

This technique is useful when you are feeling anxious or fearful. It is so much easier to deal with whatever arises when you are in a calm or relaxed state. If you use this technique in a public place, it is quite okay to keep your eyes open.

This effective exercise takes only 18 seconds. Practice it 3 times a day and whenever you have a sudden need to attain calm.

Cross Over Anti-Anxiety Technique

1. Sit or stand, and hold anything that is handy, like keys or a cellphone, in your right hand. With the object in your hand, stretch both arms out in front of you at an outward angle.
2. Move your right arm across an imaginary line that runs down the center of your body. Then place the object in the palm of the left hand.
3. Move the right arm back to its former position.
4. Move your left arm over the mid line and place the object in the palm of your right hand.
5. Move the left hand back to its former position.
6. Repeat the process for a minute or two.

By moving both arms across the mid line, both hemispheres of the brain become activated, resulting in greater blood flow and increased electrical impulses within the brain. This brings on a more tranquil and peaceful state of mind.

Calming Display Technique

Somewhere in your home or at your place of work, arrange and display a small collection of photos and mementos of some of the good times you have had. Within this arrangement, also place anything symbolic of peace and tranquility. You might also want to include small plants and herbs. This display can be your calming corner or your peaceful place.

When you are feeling stressed or uneasy spend a few

moments looking at your personal display; the photos, mementos and symbols will evoke within you feelings of tranquility and calm.

The Relaxing Aroma Technique

When inhaling the aroma in essential oils, the aroma goes via the olfactory nerve to the portion of the brain where emotions and moods are initiated. Because of the existence of this pathway, aromatherapy is able to promote relaxation and a positive state of mind. These benefits may also be experienced when the essential oils are applied in the form of creams and body lotions.

Keep a small container of the aroma-filled essential oils handy for when you need them. Visit a store carrying aromatherapy supplies and select the aroma most effective for you.

Chapter 8

Progressive Muscle Relaxer

"Take a rest; a field that has rested gives a bountiful crop."

Herodotus

Each one of us is the best expert on ourselves. We are aware of the times when our bodies cry out to us saying "I'm spent and I need to rest, relax and re-energize," or "my body is so tensed up."

Rapid relaxation relief for your body can be achieved by practicing the following technique:

Progressive Muscle Relaxer

This technique involves tensing up and then relaxing the muscles in each region of your body. To achieve maximum effect, work on each of the muscle groups, one at a time.

1. Sit or lie down in a comfortable position. A quiet area is best.

2. Take a deep breath through your nose, and then slowly exhale through your mouth.

3. Hands and Fingers: Tightly clench your hands and fingers for five seconds and as you let go and relax, say "Relaxed" or "Relaxing Now."

4. Forearms: Tense your forearms and push them

outwards against an invisible force. After five seconds, let them relax while saying "Relaxed" or "Relaxing Now."

5. Upper Arms: Bend your elbows and make your upper arms as tense as you can. After five seconds let go and as they relax say "Relaxed" or "Relaxing Now."

6. Shoulders: Scrunch up your shoulders towards the sides of your head. After five seconds, let go and as they relax say "Relaxed" or "Relaxing Now."

7. Face: Scrunch and tighten every muscle in your face for five seconds, then let go and as your face relaxes say "Relax" or "Relaxing Now."

8. Forehead: Scrunch and wrinkle up your forehead as much as you can for five seconds, then let go and as your forehead relaxes say "Relax" or "Relaxing Now."

9. Back: Tighten up your back muscles, then after five seconds let them relax and as they relax say "Relax" or "Relaxing Now."

10. Stomach: Flex your stomach muscles. Then let them relax and as they relax say "Relax" or "Relaxing Now."

11. Hips and Seat: Tighten these muscles for five seconds, and then let them relax, saying "Relax" or "Relaxing Now."

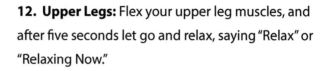

12. Upper Legs: Flex your upper leg muscles, and after five seconds let go and relax, saying "Relax" or "Relaxing Now."

13. Lower Legs: Tighten up your lower leg muscles, and after five seconds let go and relax saying "Relax" or "Relaxing Now."

14. Feet and Toes: Curl up your feet and toes as tightly as you can. After five seconds let go and relax saying "Relax" or "Relaxing Now."

Having relaxed all of your muscle groups, feel and sense calm and tranquility within your body.

Note:
You don't have to follow the exact order of the tensing and relaxing sequence. Some prefer doing this technique with their eyes closed.

To promote a more relaxed mind and body, practice this technique about three times per week and whenever needed. It only takes about three minutes to do, and for that tiny investment of your time, you are likely to notice a difference.

CAUTION:
Only tense up healthy muscles. Do not practice this technique if you have high blood pressure or other cardiovascular issues.

Chapter 9

Help with Anxiety

"Our anxiety does not empty tomorrow of its sorrows, but only empties today of its strengths."
                                                        Robert H. Spurgeon

Anxiety is an uncomfortable feeling of fear and stress. It is a common response to many of life's events and situations, like taking a test, going on a job interview, or focusing on the uncertainties of the future.

Everyone feels some mild anxiety symptoms at different times in their lives. This mild anxiety is what keeps us moving, makes us aware of dangers, and helps motivate us to find solutions to problems and reach our goals. However, when the anxiety level is high and occurs often enough to adversely affect our daily lives, corrective action is best be taken to eliminate or, at least, reduce it. If the anxiety requires it, consult a medical professional.

There are several types of anxieties. Some of these, including social anxieties and panic attacks are addressed in this book.

Suggestions to decrease anxiety:
- Use relaxation techniques, some of which are in this book, to give you tranquility and calm. These techniques can help you deal with the demands and stresses that might come your way. See Chapter 7 – Quick and Easy Relaxation Techniques, and Chapter 8 – Progressive Muscle Relaxer.

- Replace negative self-talk with positive coping talk. See Chapter 40 – Throw Out Self-doubt & Negative Thoughts.

- When anyone or anything causes you to become anxious, fearful or worried, empower yourself with the following reality check: ask yourself if that person or thing can bite your head off. If they can't bite your head off, then you will still have your mind. With your mind intact, and using some of the tools found in this book, you will be able to better hold your ground, decrease your anxiety, fears and worries and move on.

- Exercise, even if it's just a brief walk, and benefit from its mood-lifting effect. See Chapter 33 – Be a Mover.

- Increase your knowledge about the cause of your anxiety. The more you know about it and the more you see things in their real perspective, the less vulnerable you become. See Chapter 44 – Better Perceptions—Better Life.

- A state of anxiety has the inconvenient habit of, without warning, bringing into our minds, all manner of other anxiety producing thoughts. These other thoughts are often unrelated to the initial thought that sparked the anxiety and, in real life, they are most times of little or no consequence. However, in the anxious mind, they become prominent and turn into energy-sapping monsters. They grow in size and ferocity until they leave us devoid of

logic and feeling exhausted.

- Knowledge and understanding are power, so being aware of what these other thoughts are, how they behave, and what they cause, places you in a better position to immediately "pop" or ignore them before they can do you harm.

- Watching television can be a great help when you are feeling anxious about an issue. Focus your attention on the television screen to rapidly bring you into the present. Doing this will give your mind a beneficial break from its wanderings into the negative areas of the past or the uncertainty of the future. At these times, only watch comedies, cartoons, interesting documentaries and other shows with a positive message. Shows incorporating anger and violence are best avoided because they tend to prompt the subconscious to reconnect to past anxious events which can easily compound your current anxiety.

- Spending time helping others helps take the focus off yourself and your anxieties. See Chapter 23 – Helping Is a Win-Win – Why Wait?

- A constructive way to deal with anxiety is to gradually, one step at a time, expose yourself to whatever causes it. Do this and you will often find that the cause was not as big or as frightening as you had thought it to be. In fact, you might even find that you were anxious about something that did not even exist!

- Talk with a supportive person.

Chapter 10

Tame Panic Attacks

"Panic is a sudden desertion of us, and a going over to the enemy of our imagination."   *Christian Nestell Bovee*

When you suffer a panic attack, it can feel as if everything is collapsing all around you, that you are going crazy and might even die.

The good news is that the world around you is not collapsing. You only imagine that it is. You are not going crazy, and you are not about to die.

Let me remind you of four common symptoms of a panic attack:
- Increased heartbeat
- Increased rate of breathing
- Increased inflow of adrenaline
- Breaking out in a sweat

Now consider this: when you are exercising in a gym or out running, exactly the same symptoms occur. In those situations, you don't think you are going crazy, losing control or are possibly going to die. If you acknowledge and remember these facts, then the "out of control" and "about to die" feelings that you imagine and experience during a panic attack will decrease.

More techniques for decreasing panic attacks:
- At the onset of an attack, take a deep breath, tense up every muscle in your body for about 8 seconds, and then relax all of your muscles as you slowly exhale.

- Besides or in addition to the usual symptoms of a panic attack, you might become dizzy and disoriented. To ground yourself, hold onto a solid piece of furniture, a pole, a door post or whatever else is stable and will support you.

- When next you feel an attack is coming on, you can take the philosophic approach to minimize its threat by saying something like, "Oh well, it's just one of those things again, and soon it will be gone." Then let it wash right over you until it has faded away.

- When you feel that a panic attack is about to come on, close your mouth and breathe through your nose. This works because it's almost impossible to hyperventilate when breathing through your nose.

- If crowded areas like shopping centers or busy stores trigger panic attacks, consider visiting them during their slower hours.

- Another way to reduce "crowd-induced" panic attacks is to use the Gradual Exposure Technique. Begin by visiting the area or stores when there are very few visitors. After that, and within your own comfort zone, gently expose yourself to gradually increasing crowds.

Chapter 11

Patience, Anger, and Wounding Words

"Anger is a word which blows out the lamp of the mind."

Robert G. Ingersoll

Don't be deceived into thinking that being patient or being able to control one's anger are passive activities. On the contrary, these are very proactive, purposeful and essential forms of self-discipline which will not only serve you well, but will also make life more pleasant for those with whom you come into contact.

Ways to achieve patience and manage anger:

•   Give deep thought to the possibility that your impatience and anger might be, intentionally or unintentionally, inflicting harm on those around you. If unsure give them the benefit of the doubt. Also, ask yourself if you would like anyone to inflict their impatience and anger on you—treat other people as you would like to be treated.

•   Remind yourself that impatience and anger cause you to have increasingly higher stress levels, which in turn can cause you emotional and physical harm. Do you really want to cause yourself harm?

•   When you feel you are about to lose your patience and exhibit anger, place the tips of your thumb and index finger together, take a deep breath through your nose, and exhale slowly through your mouth. Simple techniques can produce rapid results!

- When possible, politely excuse yourself, and leave the room or immediate vicinity. Being in another location, away from the heat of a possible confrontation, will make it easier to consciously and carefully consider your response.

- Responding in a calm and quiet manner is likely to have a calming effect on the other person. If the location allows, calm the situation down further by offering the person somewhere to sit and a refreshment.

- For the following reason, controlling anger is extremely important: when we are angry, we are more likely to insult or put this person down. Even if the words we use in anger are not meant to cause damage, they often do. The nursery rhyme "sticks and stones will break my bones, but words will never hurt me," is not true.

Words can be
wounding weapons!

Damage caused by sticks and stones can be repaired in a doctor's office or in the ER, but the damage and hurt caused by words, especially if they are repeated, can deeply wound, cripple or cause emotional stress to a person, not just temporarily, but for years to come. You would be astounded at the large amount of people whose self-esteem was damaged because at some point in their lives they were wrongly told that they were worthless or useless or something equally unkind. Those damaging words become ingrained in a person's subconscious, giving rise to the false truths about who a person now believes himself to be. This ultimately results in the development of negative thought patterns which will often cause the occurrence of unproductive and negative behavior.

Chapter 12

Preventing Emailing and Texting Anger

"Speak when you are angry and you will make the best speech you will ever regret."
Ambrose Bierce

Today technological advances allow us to communicate with methods other than speech. Our thoughts and frame of mind influence how we respond, so whether we are speaking, emailing or texting, it is best to do so thoughtfully and calmly so that our human values remain intact.

If you receive an email or text message that makes you angry, refuse to immediately reply. Give yourself a chance to calm down. Use the 18-Second Relaxing Technique in Chapter 7 – Quick and Easy Relaxation Techniques. Only when you feel composed, think about

how you will reply. When considering your reply, bear in mind that texts and emails do not have tones in the way that voices do. Therefore your interpretation of the message might not be in line with the way it was intended. If there is something in the message that you don't fully understand, ask the sender for clarification to take care of any misunderstanding. Unless you are having a humorous exchange with someone who is more than just an acquaintance, email and text messages are not the best ways to use sarcasm or humor. They could be taken up in a way that you never intended, possibly causing a problem or making an already bad situation worse.

In times past, the modes of communication between parties were slower, giving them more time to consider their responses. Now messages go back and forth much faster and, if a message angers us, we might not pause long enough to give it due thought and consideration, but rather we respond in anger without regard of possible consequences. The following can help prevent this reaction.

On-Paper-Vent Method

Before responding, do this: write down all the stuff you want to say on an actual piece of paper. Allow yourself to vent, be as damning as you wish. Read your response several times until you get your anger or upset fully out of your system. Then place the paper in a drawer.

Type-The-Address-Last Method

To prevent accidentally sending your response before you are totally satisfied with it, I suggest you use the Type-The-Address-Last Method. This is the sequence: calm down, type your response, walk away from it, take a break, read it again, make only necessary edits and when you are satisfied with it, then and only then type in the recipient's address and send it off.

Consider having someone who is emotionally detached from the subject matter of the email give his or her objective view.

The time taken to carefully and thoughtfully compose an email or text message takes much less time than the time it takes to undo and repair the damage caused by a rage-tainted email or text. Not to be forgotten is the emotional and relationship damage caused by keyboard rages.

Emailing and texting rapid, impulse-charged back-and-forth responses often deteriorate into senseless shootouts. After the shootout is over and you are feeling relaxed, read through the texts and see what was actually achieved. In all likelihood, you will probably conclude that nothing was achieved. Worse, in some cases, you might find that even if it was unintentional, damage was caused emotionally or materially.

CAUTION: Once you have hit "send" there is no way you can reach out and bring back your reply. It is already well on its non-stop flight to Harmsville. Take the time to really think about your response. You do not want to regret your action, especially if it could have a negative impact on you now or in the future.

In our instant world, we send an email or a text and expect an immediate reply and if that doesn't happen we might become frustrated and even angry. Well guess what, none of us owns that kind of total control over anybody. In most cases, no one has to respond immediately, though exceptions to this could include emergencies and certain work situations. As an email or text sender, bear in mind that maybe the other party mislaid their phone, maybe the communication equipment where they live is down, maybe they are in a class, there are so many valid reasons for not replying immediately. It also could be that the other person needs time to consider a response.

Chapter 13

Instant Mind Vacation

"The art of resting the mind and the power of dismissing from it all care and worry is probably one of the secrets of our great men."   *Captain J.A. Hatfield*

When our bodies feel tired we rest for a while. When our minds tire they too need to rest.

A quick and easy, yet very effective way to rest and relax your mind is to treat it to a vacation. This vacation does not involve booking a hotel, waiting in lines at airports or taking long car journeys. This Instant Mind Vacation allows you to give your mind a break whenever you choose—even during your busy work day!

The basic steps to taking an Instant Mind Vacation:

1. Sit or lie down in a place where you will not be disturbed.

2. Close your eyes, take a deep breath, and allow yourself to drift off to any place where you find peace, calm, and tranquility. This can be on a beach, by a river, in a forest, a garden, a mountain top or anywhere you choose.

3. Once you are there, use some or all of your senses, and allow yourself to:

- See what you see there.
- Hear what you hear there.
- Feel what you feel there.
- Smell what you smell there.
- Taste what you taste there.

When daydreaming, our minds tend to wander about, but with this technique you take a proactive and purposeful role. You deliberately enhance your presence at your chosen vacation spot by noticing and experiencing all that you see, hear, feel, smell, and taste there. If you can't access every sense, that's okay.

Here is a more detailed example, assuming you have chosen a beach as your vacation spot:

Read the next 10 steps and the notes that follow before performing step 1.

1. Close your eyes, take a deep breath, let your imagination flow and be at the beach.

2. Step onto the beach and feel the warm sand under your feet.

3. Hear the crunch of the sand as you walk leisurely towards the water.

4. See or imagine the ocean, which can be any shade of blue you choose.

5. Observe the waves breaking on the shore. Each wave takes you deeper into rest and relaxation.

6. Feel the sea breeze as it gently touches your skin.

7. Smell the saltiness in the air.

8. See or imagine the trees and other vegetation surrounding the beach. If there are flowers there, they can be any color you want them to be.

9. Visualize the sky, which might be clear and blue, or hazy and cloudy.

10. After several minutes, or however long you choose the vacation to be, slowly open your eyes and return feeling rested and relaxed.

Notes: The mind vacation described above is only an example. You can customize it in any way to suit your desires.

You can change your choice of destination whenever you wish and then easily fill in the scene in your mind.

If, in the beginning, you have some difficulty using this technique, don't worry, start in a small way and you will improve with practice. Don't force anything to happen. Just want it to happen and let it happen.

Use this technique whenever you feel your mind needs a break, or whenever you would just like to "get away."

Your Own Private Sanctuary

You can also think of your chosen place, be it a beach or a garden, etc. as being your own private sanctuary, a place where you can go, whenever you wish, to immerse yourself in its tranquility and to recharge. It is your space; other people may only enter your space with your permission.

CAUTION: Do not practice this Instant Vacation Mind technique, or anything similar to it, while driving a vehicle, while operating or being in the proximity of any kind of machinery, or whenever alertness is needed.

Chapter 14

Live In The Now

"Live now, believe me wait not till tomorrow, gather the roses of life today."

Pierre De Ronsard

You can live in any one of three places, the Past, the Now, or the Future. The Past has gone and will never come back. All The Past has to offer are memories and lessons.

The Future is usually a place filled with anxiety and worry, but it does not serve you well to worry. Mark Twain said, *"I have had a lot of worries in my life, most of which never happened."* Sensible planning is wise, but worrying about the future is not very productive. When you are in The Now and focused on the moment, you are not distracted and bogged down by thoughts of The Past or The Future. This allows for your creativity and productivity to move into a higher gear, enabling you to achieve your goals more easily and more efficiently.

How to live in The Now:

• Express gratitude for what you have

Stop for a moment and express gratitude for what you have. Experience how this simple act can transport you into The Now . Make a list of your assets and of those people close to you.

• Be appreciative of what you are able to do

Take a deep breath of fresh air and exhale. Now think of those who for some medical reason cannot inhale and exhale as easily as you just did. The act of appreciating what you are able to do, especially while you are performing the action, immediately brings you into The Now.

• Be in The Now while eating

Mindfully savor your food. Chew slowly and consciously. Deliberately taste and appreciate each and every mouthful. Doing this allows you to experience The Present and be in The Now. An added bonus of this technique is that it allows for better and healthier digestion.

• Stop and Observe

1. At a convenient time, stop what you are doing and observe your surroundings.

2. See everything you see, hear everything you hear, feel all that you feel and smell what you smell. By intently tuning into your senses and being consciously aware of your breathing, you simultaneously become more conscious of your inner self and your surroundings. This process immerses you in The Now and enables you to better experience the richness and fullness of the present moment. This technique can also be used to rapidly ground yourself.

Practice these "Being in The Now" techniques as often as you can. When you live in The Now you appreciate and savor each moment and life becomes much more vibrant and enjoyable. See Chapter 57 - More Mindful Methods in Minutes.

Chapter 15

Harboring Hate and Revenge

"Something of vengeance I had tasted for the first time; as romantic wine it seemed, on swallowing, warm and racy: its after-flavor, metallic and corroding, gave me a sensation as if I had been poisoned."
                                                            Charlotte Bronte

Harboring hate and revenge might seem appropriate and comforting, but they serve no real beneficial purpose. In fact, hate and revenge achieve the opposite results. As long as you have a cauldron of hate and revenge boiling inside you, it is only you, the hater, who suffers. The person for whom you feel this hate is going about his or her daily life, totally unaware of the discomfort that is eating at you from the inside out. It is much more constructive to channel the energy spent on hating into something positive both for you and for others around you.

The person carrying the hate.

The other person.

You lose a lot of valuable time and joy by hating others and plotting your revenge. Reject this self-destructive, no-win path and find solutions to overcome it.

• If there is someone you hate and you spend time and energy thinking about them, write down exactly what you think you are going to gain by hating him or her and by plotting your revenge against them. From what you have written you will see that, besides from it possibly allowing you to feel a little sorry for yourself, there is ZERO to gain and much to lose.

Hatred is a boomerang which is sure to hit you harder than the person you threw it at.

Author Unknown

• A proven, time-tested solution to overcoming hate is forgiveness. More about this in Chapter 16 – The Power and Benefits of Forgiving.

You will become a much happier person when all the hate is out of your system.

Chapter 16

The Power and Benefits of Forgiving

"Only the brave know how to forgive, it is the most refined and generous pitch of human virtue human nature can arrive at."

Laurence Sterne

Forgiving is an act of strength, whereby you as the "forgiver" offers a gift of mercy.

Forgiving is not a weakness because you are not excusing or condoning the behavior that harmed you. Forgiving is a conscious decision to let go of resentments and thoughts of revenge in order to move on and live your life to the fullest. Forgiving people for the harm they caused you will free your mind from negative thoughts and continually festering wounds, allowing you to take back full control of your life. Until you forgive the people who have wronged you, they will continue to have control and be a powerful influence over you. The negative thoughts you have towards them deplete your own positive energy and erode your peace of mind.

Additional benefits of forgiveness:
It is widely accepted in the medical and psychology professions that forgiveness can lead to many benefits including the following:

- Greater peace of mind
- Higher self-esteem and confidence
- Lower blood pressure
- Stronger immune system
- Less anxiety and stress

Professional Psychology reported that in a study of clients being counseled, therapists who utilized specific forgiveness interventions were more successful than those who did not.

It is most important to note that many of the people who hurt people have themselves, at some time in their lives, been hurt by other people. This fact is very clearly described by the expression: **"Hurt People, Hurt People."** You don't have to spend any time psychoanalyzing the wrongdoer, nor is it necessary to know all the details of that person's past. It is sufficient to know that the person who is hurtful toward you is most probably doing so out of his own hurt, insecurities and fears.

Since we have not walked a mile in the shoes of the wrongdoers and have not experienced all that they have gone through in their own lives, it is not for us to judge or condemn them, but rather to have compassion and forgive. **Please note that forgiveness does not require that you have to let the person who hurt you back into your life. You can forgive and still decide that it is best for you to remain physically and emotionally distanced from the person who harmed you.**

Schoolyard bullies have often been hurt or neglected. To release their hurt and gain a sense of power and self-importance, bullies pick on and attack those whom they see as physically or emotionally weaker than them. Showing the bully compassion might put an end to his or her bad behavior, because deep down what most bullies crave is care and positive attention.

The benefits of forgiving are too important to ignore—every night before going to sleep, think of all those who have harmed you that day; forgive them and let it go—it will free you.

It is vitally essential to note that once you have forgiven the abuser, it is most important that you forgive yourself for having carried the burden and the pain for as long as you did. Don't forget to do this.

"Forgiving is the key that unlocks and releases endless resentment, bitterness and thoughts of revenge towards others. For their sake and for your sake – TURN THE KEY."

Adapt. C. ten Boom

FORGIVENESS

Chapter 17

Overcoming Grief

"While grief is fresh, every attempt to divert it only irritates. You must wait till grief be digested, and then amusement will dissipate the remains of it."   Samuel Johnson

After losing someone close to you, there is a time to grieve. If you find that rituals and customs help you with your grieving, then observe and practice them.

Additional ways to overcome grief:

- Donate money, goods or time to a cause he supported. This will help facilitate the continuation of his good work and celebrate his life and values.

- Return to work and your normal routine as soon as a possible. Become involved in your interests and hobbies, and if you don't have any, this can be the right time to start one. Doing so will help redirect your focus away from your grieving.

- Don't hold all of your emotions in, this will do you no good and only prolong the grieving process. If there is something you wanted to tell the person, but for whatever reason did not or could not—close your eyes, imagine the person to be in your presence or within earshot and, from your heart, speak the words you wanted to tell him or her.

- **The Conversation**

This conversation has played a role in helping prevent my clients from **turning a season of grieving into a lifetime of mourning.**

Me: How are you feeling today about the loss of_____?

Client: Mostly sad, but also fearful and anxious at times.

Me: Close your eyes and imagine or pretend that _____ is close to you right now. Can you do that?

Client: Yes.

Me: In that case, what would _____ be saying to you right now?

Client: Stop feeling so sad, go out and enjoy yourself.

Me: How does that sound to you?

Client: Sounds good.

Me: How would _____ react if you carried on being sad and didn't go out and enjoy yourself?

Client: _____ would be upset with me.

Me: Do you want _____ to be upset with you?

Client: No.

Me: So, then what are you going to do?

Client: I'm going to do what _____ would want and expect me to do, and to get on with my life, enjoy myself, and have a good time.

The following poem "*Gone From My Sight*" by Henry Van Dyke has given comfort and light to many who have lost someone close:

Gone From My Sight

I am standing upon the seashore.

A ship at my side spreads her white sails to the moving breeze
and starts for the blue ocean.
She is an object of beauty and strength,
and I stand and watch her until, at length she hangs
like a speck of white cloud
just where the sea and sky come to mingle with each other.
Then someone at my side says,
"There she goes!"
Gone where?
Gone from my sight...that is all.
She is just as large in mast, hull and spar
as she was when she left my side
and she is just as able to bear her load of living freight

to her destined port.

Her diminished size is in me, not in her.

And just at the moment

when someone says,

"There, she is gone,"

there are other eyes watching her coming…

and other voices ready to take up the glad shout,…

"Here she comes!"

Chapter 18

Deciding What Is Really Important

"Things which matter most must never be at the mercy of things which matter least."   *Johann W. von Goethe*

We often spend too much time and energy on relatively unimportant matters.

You can stop this habit by giving each negative issue or event a number.

1. Draw a vertical line about eight inches tall.

2. Number the line 1-10. Start at the bottom, equally spacing the numbers.

Write down → the worst thing that could happen

10. _____
9. _____
8. _____
7. _____
6. _____
5. _____
4. _____
3. _____
2. _____
1. _____

Write down other things that are not as serious as what you wrote at the 10 level

3. Beside #10, write down the most awful thing that could happen to you or your family. Examples could be a bad accident or your house burning down.

4. Now, think of events like spilling food onto your slacks, scratching your new shoes, a dent on your car or other things that upset and annoy you.

5. Take a look at the numbered vertical line and give each one of these issues from Step 4 a number in comparison to the gravity and severity of the really bad event you assigned to the #10. I bet you gave them all numbers pretty close to the bottom of the vertical line showing how unimportant they really are. **By simply assigning a number to any event compared to the worst-case #10 event, you can see how this technique rapidly enables you to acquire a new perspective and place a correct value on a current event in terms of its severity and importance in your life.**

So the next time you step into a puddle and wet your new shoes, or your sweater gets caught on a nail and a thread or two is pulled, just assign the event a number in relation to the worst possible event and feel the annoyance subside.

Viewing issues and events in a priority perspective will spare you frustration, anger and aggravation. It is also gratifying to know that most of the issues to which you assign low numbers can be easily repaired or replaced.

What matters is being able to decide the relative importance of the issues and events in our lives and knowing how to prevent them from unnecessarily and negatively affecting us.

Chapter 19

Overwhelmed? Conquer it

"The older I get, the more wisdom I find in the ancient rule of taking first things first—a process which often reduces the most complex human problems to manageable proportions."

Dwight D. Eisenhower

We often find ourselves overwhelmed by the sheer magnitude of a single task, or by having to attend to many differing tasks in a short span of time.

These situations can easily cause stress, and even paralyze us in our tracks. This leads to inaction, which, leads to even more stress and anxiety.

The following techniques will help you:

Step Backwards Technique

This technique is based on the fact that when you walk backwards and away from a large object, like a mountain, it becomes smaller and less daunting.

Close your eyes and visualize or imagine a huge, overwhelming mountain right in front of you. Let's call it Mount Overwhelm. Now, observe what happens when you imagine yourself walking backwards and away from the mountain. The mountain becomes smaller, less daunting and therefore less overwhelming.

Now, with your eyes closed, picture or imagine the huge task you have to complete. It looks so huge and overpowering—it is your Mount Overwhelm. Next, imagine walking backwards and away from your mountainous-looking task. As you do, it will appear smaller, less overwhelming, and therefore more manageable.

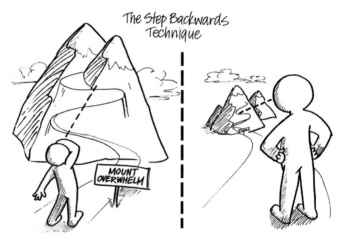

The purpose of this Step Backwards Technique is to put you at your ease by making the mountainous task appear smaller. When you are feeling at ease and relaxed, you are more prepared to take on and complete even the biggest tasks.

Smaller Pieces Technique
Another really effective technique to prevent you from becoming overwhelmed is to cut Mount Overwhelm into smaller more manageable pieces. When that is done, work on and complete one piece at a time.

The completion of each piece allows you more opportunities for victories and for the feelings of accomplishment that come with each of those victories!

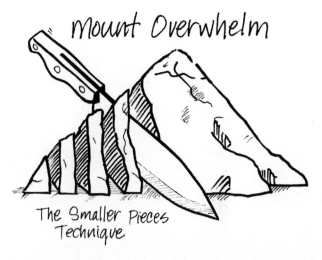

mount Overwhelm

The Smaller Pieces Technique

It is most important to note that your efficiency is higher when attending to one piece of the mountain at a time, rather than multitasking and attending to all of the pieces of the mountain at the same time.

Priority Technique

When you have many differing tasks to complete in a limited amount of time, prioritizing them will help you rapidly achieve order and prevent you from becoming overwhelmed.

On a piece of paper draw a simple figure of yourself juggling a number of balls, with each ball representing a different task. Next to each ball, write a brief description of each task. Next, in order of the priority of each task, assign a number to each ball. The ball associated with the task that must be completed first will be assigned the number one, the ball associated with the task that will be completed next will be assigned the number two and so on.

Complete task number one and then take a short break. In order of priority, move onto the next task until they are all completed.

Again, paying your full attention to one matter at a time is more efficient than multitasking.

Chapter 20

Commitment, Drive and Motivation

"For purposes of action, nothing is more useful than focus of thought combined with energy of will."

Henri Frederick Amiel

Tips and techniques to commit, drive and motivate yourself:

- Be specific and decide exactly what it is that you want to do or accomplish. Your goal must be reasonable and believable. If not, you could be setting yourself up for failure.

- Write down the reasons why it is important for you to accomplish your goal. When you know why it is important to accomplish your goal, then, and only then, will you really commit and apply the required passion and determination to achieve it. To help charge yourself up, read your reasons for accomplishing this goal at least three times per day.

- Be prepared to step out of your comfort zone. Be ready and prepared to make the necessary sacrifices to succeed.

- Realize that unexpected obstacles will arise, but that somehow you will figure out a way to overcome them. Where there is a will there is a way!

- When your self-belief needs a lift, close your eyes and recall a previous success of yours. If you say that you do not have a success to recall, let me remind you of a success that you once had, and have probably forgotten all about. Go back to the time when you were still a baby sitting on the floor and you wanted to stand up. You probably grabbed a table leg or the chair and attempted to pull yourself up. You fell, but you pulled yourself up again. This routine of pulling yourself up after falling down occurred several times until you finally mastered the art of standing. Just as you succeeded then, you can succeed now!!

- Acquire the knowledge needed to reach your goal by educating yourself, or consulting with experts.

- Visually remind yourself of your goal by placing words and pictures to support your motivation and success in strategic places so you will often see them. The more you see them, the more they enter into your subconscious and the more your passion and motivation will grow.

- Close your eyes for a few minutes, take a deep breath and visualize or imagine yourself succeeding—your subconscious believes what you visualize as being actual and then plays its part in helping you achieve your goals. While visualizing, feel throughout your body whatever you believe or imagine success to feel like. The feeling could be a light feeling, a tingling feeling or whatever feeling works for you. Intensify that feeling. Include in this visualization any sounds, smells and tastes that you associate with success. Repeat this technique twice or more a day.

- An inspiring example of goal-oriented motivation is the story of

Sylvester Stallone's Rocky Balboa character in the movie "Rocky". He was totally motivated to succeed. He gave it his all. He trained with total passion, focus and unwavering determination. He did whatever was necessary to succeed. If you follow Rocky's example, your chances of success will increase. Passion, drive and total dedication combine to make a powerful and winning combination!

- Inspire yourself to greater heights of motivation by watching an inspirational movie that appeals to you. As you might guess from the last bullet, I have found the movie "Rocky," to be extremely motivational and have watched it many times.

- Music is also a powerful mood enhancer and motivator. The "Rocky" theme song, "Gonna Fly Now," is almost as inspirational and motivational to me as the movie itself. Choose a song or piece of music that inspires you and makes you feel like a winner. Make that song your "motivational anthem"— listen to it especially when you need a boost, it will help drive you to greater heights!

- Once you have decided to go ahead with your project, press your "start button" and go for it. Be aware of and feel the sense of accomplishment that your initial steps forward give you. Celebrate your progress. Having tasted and savored your successful start, acknowledge to yourself that the complete accomplishment of your goal is now attainable. Like a laser beam, sharply focus all of your reasons to succeed, all of your of abilities and all of your determination on your goal. Be unstoppable.

The Big Five

My clients have found that writing down the answers to the following five questions is a huge help in clearly defining what must be done to achieve their goals. If reaching your goal is what you want, I strongly suggest you do the same!

- How will I benefit when I reach my goal?
- What do I have to do less of to reach my goal?
- What do I have to stop doing to reach my goal?
- What do I have to do more of to reach my goal?
- What else do I need to do to reach my goal?

Results and change happen, not by wishing and not by hoping, but only by determined, passionate, motivated and relentless doing.

Chapter 21

Choices and Decisions

"To know just what has to be done, then to do it, comprises the whole philosophy of practical life."   Sir William Osler

We are often confronted with having to make choices. Choices can be simple, like deciding where to go for dinner, or they can be more complex, like whether or not to take up a new position in another state. Making a choice, or even just the thought of making a choice can be daunting or time-consuming, or both. The following techniques can help you with your choice making.

Realization Technique

You choose what clothes to wear, which emails to delete, or what TV shows to watch. You choose what to have for breakfast and what time to go to sleep. The realization that you make choices and decisions all day long will help you when the bigger choices come along.

Pros vs. Cons Technique

1. A lifestyle-making choice, such as dieting, would best be made by first writing down all the pros and cons, and giving each due consideration.

2. Clearly make a point of stressing all the negative consequences of not making the choice that would serve you best.

3. You are now in a good position to make your choice. Always bear in mind that if the choice being made is not a matter of life or death, you can always readjust it later. Being a little on the bold side will always speed up your decision-making process.

Deep Communication Technique

1. Go to a quiet area and make yourself comfortable.

2. Close your eyes, take a deep breath, and let your body relax.

3. Think of a person or power you consider wise and who has your best interests at heart.

4. Communicate with this person, power, or your own higher self in whatever way you like. Ask what they would suggest about your current dilemma.

5. Having taken notice of their advice, and also taking

into account your personal views, this could be the right time to make your choice.

Notes: It is best not to engage in the choice-making process when your emotions are running high. All too often, our emotions push aside or reduce our sense of reason and logical thinking. Postpone your decision-making until you are at your logical best and have had enough time to consider all the options.

Don't procrastinate on your decision-making since this could easily result in lost opportunities and other negative impacts.

Make a list of what the long term effects of your current choices and decisions might be. This is a vitally important part of the decision-making process.

If your choice or decision requires the researching of information, verify as best you can that the information is correct and unbiased. Don't waste your time and energy in second guessing. Once you have made your choice, let it go.

Some people will opt not to make a choice because they don't want to be committed to following through. This is often out of a fear of failing or not wanting to look foolish if they don't succeed. See Chapter 26 – Conquer the Fear of Failure, for advice in dealing with these issues.

In life, the more rewarding choice is rarely the easy choice, but the easy choice is rarely ever the right choice.

Chapter 22

Overcoming Procrastination Today!

"Nothing is as fatiguing as the eternal hanging on of an uncompleted task."
                                        William James

We procrastinate, and in addition to the stress and worry caused by the non-completion of a task, we berate ourselves for being lazy, which does little for our self-esteem and confidence. Procrastination is often a cause of insomnia. We are awoken during the night and kept awake for varying periods by thoughts from our subconscious mind constantly reminding us of the work that still needs to be done.

Procrastination solutions:

• Don't over-think the task…this will cause "Analysis Paralysis" and nothing will get done.

• Make a to-do list of your most important chores, and complete them one at a time in order of priority.

• Fear of failure is a cause of procrastination. See Chapter

26 – Conquer the Fear of Failure.

• If you don't know how to do something, find out how.

• Break up a task into manageable segments.

• Reward yourself with something, like a cup of coffee, after completing each segment.

• Motivate yourself to complete a task by closing your eyes, taking a deep breath and then feel the feeling of how good you will feel when you have completed the task.

• Fear that you will not produce a perfect result is often a cause of procrastination. See Chapter 25 – You Don't Have to Be Perfect.

• Make a list of the unpleasant consequences of not completing the task on time.

• Do the toughest tasks when you have the most energy.

• Remove all distractions from your work area.

• Be acutely aware of when you are spending too much time on a particular detail or are being side-tracked in any way. Come back to focusing on the task at hand.

• Ask a mentor or someone else to help keep you on schedule.

• Make yourself socially accountable. Tell your friends or family what you intend to do or achieve and by when. That way, people you care about are expecting to see you execute a task in a certain time. This is good pressure!

• Many people sit around on the sidelines waiting for the perfect moment to start a project. For some, that perfect moment comes too late, or worse, for others it never comes at all. You see, there often is no perfect moment. Rather than sitting on the sidelines, wasting precious time, be out there now—learning, doing and achieving.

• Don't delay because you are not totally equipped. Consider starting an assignment with just the tools you have. Improvise if you have to, and pleasantly surprise yourself with your innovation!

• Take a 10 minute walk every 50 minutes. This will refresh your mind and re-energize you for the next task.

• If you have a novel idea and procrastinate in bringing it to the market, you might well lose out to someone who has the same idea but who immediately swings into action. Let the thought of this happening deter you from procrastinating when you get your big idea!

Chapter 23

Helping is a Win-Win—Why Wait?

"Wherever there is a human being, there is an opportunity for a kindness." Seneca

Helping others and doing volunteer work has benefits for both the givers and the receivers. Giving to charity is a good thing and it certainly does produce very beneficial results, however, it is not the only way to give. Giving your time to making human contact and offering the undivided attention of a listening ear are not only appreciated but are also rich in therapeutic value.

I often suggest to people who have self-esteem issues, or to those who complain about their lot in life, to go out and do a couple of hours of volunteer work each week. Volunteering can be done in so many different ways. It could be reading to someone with fading eyesight, tutoring a child with his homework or joining an organization that distributes food and clothing. The list of good causes is endless.

Helping activities produce five important results:

- They benefit the recipient.
- They help take the focus off the giver's own issues.
- They put a smile on the recipient's face
- They have the therapeutic effect of boosting the giver's own sense of worth and feelings of happiness.
- Helping those who are not as comparatively fortunate serves as a reminder to be grateful for what we have.

Small, spontaneous acts of kindness and caring make a big difference. If you can, keep the kindness and the caring coming,

Search the internet or ask your friends and you will find many organizations that would be happy to receive your help.

Giving help in the workplace:
In the workplace, many of us have become influenced by a belief that being a little too helpful, kind or compassionate, both towards ourselves and others might blunt our edge and impede our drive and determination to succeed. We definitely have to be hard-working and determined in order to succeed, but there is also the big picture and your contribution to the greater good to consider. By the phrase "contribution to the greater good", I mean helping and encouraging those on your team. By doing so you will empower them, their productivity will increase, the work environment will improve, and from all this you too will benefit—another example of Win-Win. Don't wait to win.

Three Good Questions

"If I am not for myself, who will be for me?

But if I am only for me, then what am I?

If not now, then when?"

Hillel

Chapter 24

Be a Thanker

"When it comes to life the critical thing is whether you take things for granted or take them with gratitude."

G.K.. Chesterton

People appreciate being recognized and thanked for their services. There are times when we are so absorbed in our own activities that we forget to be a "thanker".

Taking a few moments to say thanks and express gratitude to someone for even the smallest of services, will not only boost that person's self-esteem and motivate him or her to further improve their performance, but showing appreciation will also make you feel good. A "thank you" via email is always appreciated, but it does not match the feeling and appreciation of receiving a handwritten note. Make an investment in some cards and when it feels appropriate take a couple of minutes to write a note of thanks. Each time the recipient sees the card, his or her sense of self-worth and feeling of appreciation will receive another positive boost.

Equally as important is thanking those who pay you a compliment or thank you for your services.

When we are given compliments or acknowledgments, it is important to accept them graciously. Often we respond by saying "It was nothing. "Well, it's not "nothing." If it was nothing, the other person would not have bothered to thank or compliment us. When someone offers thanks or praise, he or she has made the conscious decision to do so; it is right to accept and respond to those words in the same manner they were given. A well-meant and sincere "thank you" is usually all that's required. Accept praise and allow it to enrich who you are. In addition, gratitude shows sensitivity and caring, and makes for better relationships.

Showing gratitude for what we have and for what we are able to do is always a good thing.
Every time you see or think of someone who is in a difficult way, the following two words can express your gratitude for what you have and for your more favorable situation:

"I'm thankful."

When you wake up in the morning, acknowledge some of the things that you are fortunate enough to have, and then think or say the words: "I'm thankful." **Doing this before you reach out for your phone to read your emails and texts will place you in a more balanced frame of mind to better manage your day.** When you turn off the light at night and you have a warm bed and a roof over your head that too is an appropriate time to say "I'm thankful."

Whenever things turn out favorably, think or say the two words "I'm thankful." It really takes no time at all.

Being thankful has several very positive effects:
- Thankfulness can have positive effects on the brain and body systems. Those systems include the systems associated with mood, social bonding, pleasure, the immune system, stress and blood

pressure. For this alone thankfulness can be described as being one of the key ingredients in the recipe for a better life!

- Being grateful for what we have decreases the habit of making negative comparisons to other people. It also minimizes any bitterness and jealousy we might be harboring.

- Appreciating and being thankful for the material possessions we already own reduces the time-wasting obsessiveness and longing we might have for things we would like, but which are currently out of our reach.

- Being grateful decreases the tendency to be self-centered, creating within us a greater sense of humility.

- Acts of gratitude promote the positive effects associated with giving and receiving. These positive effects include allowing you to experience and become immersed in the full richness of living and being in The Now. Feeling the benefits of these positive and rewarding effects makes it more likely that you will in the future again perform similar generous and thoughtful acts.

- The following might seem like a grind but the results make it well worth the doing: every day, write down what you are thankful for, just two or three things will do. It can be a sunset, a conversation you recently had, a person, anything. At the end of the week, read the entire list and you will be pleasantly surprised at how much you have to be thankful for.

- Use the tool of visual reminders. Write some of the items you are thankful for on Post-it notes and place them where you are most likely to see them several times a day. The more you see and read the notes the more appreciative you become.

Gratitude is a habit, and like any good habit, you have to keep practicing it.

Chapter 25

You Don't Have To Be Perfect

"A man would do nothing if he waited until he could do it so well that no one could find fault."   *John Henry Newman*

Perfectionism is the tendency to set unrealistically high standards for yourself.

Very little in life, except perhaps nature itself, is perfect. Despite this, some of us keep aiming for this unattainable goal. Striving to reach perfection in our challenges, goals, and projects leads to frustration, anxiety, and wear and tear on our minds and bodies. Additionally, projects are never started or are given up midway. Bearing all this in mind, it is far more beneficial for you and for those around you not to treat yourself so unfairly. Insisting on perfection ultimately serves no good purpose; rather do your very best in a reasonable time, and then move on to your next project.

At the Academy Awards®, Oscars are given out for excellence in each category, not for perfection. There is a good reason for this!

Persian carpet weavers intentionally include a small imperfection in their carpets for two good reasons: First, the imperfection keeps the weavers humble by reminding them that man with his best efforts can very rarely achieve perfection. Second, they knew they could weave more carpets in a given time when they were not concerned with attempting to produce 100% perfect products. In view of the success of their age-old industry, it is difficult not to agree with their anti-perfectionist mindset.

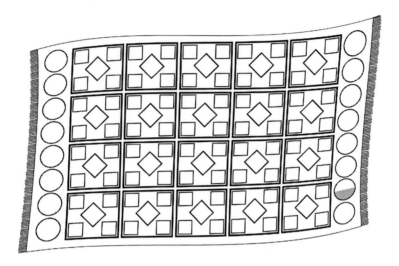

The Navajo are also skilled weavers of rugs and wall-hangings. They too incorporate a small flaw into all of their works because they believe that only their gods are capable of producing perfection. Like the Persians, the Navajo also believe it is unwise for man to insist on producing only perfect products.

Here's how to deal with perfectionism:

- **Simply replace the word "perfection"**
  Next time you have a project to accomplish, simply replace the word "perfection" with "to the very best of my ability." You will be pleased you did.

- **See the big picture: don't waste time agonizing over minor details.**

If you are not an artist, feel free to adapt the following example to your project or interest. Say you were painting a vase of flowers from out of your head, would it make any major difference to the finished painting if the vase in the painting held eleven roses or twelve roses?

This one?
That one?
This one?
That one?

Is it worth spending hours doing one sketch after the other to figure out the "perfect" number of flowers for your painting? In reality it really won't make any difference to the viewers or to the world at large. If you accept this reality, it will likely become of diminishing importance to you as well. The same applies to the details in the decorations on the vase and everything else in the painting. Don't waste your time and energy agonizing over trivial details. Besides, if you intend to complete several paintings for an upcoming show, your time-consuming quest for perfection could result in less work to exhibit at the opening. Beware! Perfectionism could also drive you to unnecessary redoes and overworking areas of the artwork. All this will culminate in a not-so-pretty painting and one unhappy artist.

"Decrease Perfection" Technique

1. At the start of your next painting (or whatever you do) session, close your eyes and visualize or imagine your habit of perfectionism taking on a shape and a color.

2. Imagine the shape transforming into a colored mist.

3. Let the mist exit your body through the pores in your skin and evaporate into the air till it's all gone. When you are feeling less or no need to attain perfection, that is a good time to take out your brushes and paints, or whatever equipment your project requires. If you want to modify this visualization to better suit yourself, go ahead. Now create!

- **Reconsider your "all or nothing" mindset and don't worry about being criticized.**

Assume that you were a perfectionist organizing a large gala dinner and the yellow flowers the florist delivered were not the exact shade of yellow you requested. So you do what many perfectionists do: you fret and worry that this shade of yellow will put an end to your plan to present perfect floral displays and because of that, the entire dinner will be a failure. Let's be practical, will the whole dinner be a failure? The truth is, it won't. Furthermore, you will probably be the only person to notice the different shade. Nobody is going to criticize you. Quite honestly, almost everybody is far too occupied with their own stuff to notice inconsequential details so you are on very safe ground. When anyone makes a negative remark to you about inconsequential details, such as the difference in the shade of yellow flowers, it is that poor individual who has the problem. Have pity for him and confidently move on knowing that in the real world, inconsequential details don't make a bit of difference. You did your very best, the guests enjoyed themselves and the dinner was a success. That's all that matters!

- **Perfectionism often begins way back.**
  When we were young, some of the words spoken to us by authoritative figures, like our parents and teachers, made lasting impressions on us. These impressions influenced our behavior. Our parents often sowed the seeds of our perfectionism when they kept telling us that we were "so awesome and so perfect," and that "because we are so smart we will achieve perfect results." When our teachers told us: "You must do better than that. Next test I expect you to produce perfect scores," not only did their words begin to ingrain in us the need to achieve perfection, but they also set in motion our fear of criticism if we did not achieve perfection. The more often we heard the words, the deeper and longer-lasting were the impressions they made in our subconscious minds, and the more of a perfectionist the child, and later the adult, became.

  One can choose to resolve this "perfection beginnings" issue by consulting a professional who is skilled in dealing with this type of situation.

- **Condition yourself to reduce your perfectionism**

  A useful conditioning exercise is to intentionally leave a couple of clothing items on a chair instead of placing them in your closet. You will soon realize that a little bit of imperfection did not cause the world to end. Or, next time you weed your garden, leave a few weeds growing in the grass. Days later you will notice that you still have a beautiful garden. In reality, it's the big picture that counts— it's the silly little inconsequential bits and pieces that just cause you to become irritable and frustrated. Ignore them, and you will find that you can quite easily succeed without them!

Want a life-changing correction? Toss out your quest for perfection.

Chapter 26

Conquer The Fear Of Failure

"To make no mistake is not in the power of man; but from their errors and mistakes the wise and good learn wisdom for the future."
                                                                    Plutarch

So many successful people have found that their failures were an integral part of the journey towards achieving their goals.

Solutions and reasons to overcome the fear of failure:

- It is most important to believe that as long as you do your best, that it is okay to fail. Sitting back and not taking a shot doesn't work for anyone. It will get you nowhere. If you fail, the constructive and optimistic approach to failing is to view failure, not as a disaster or the end of the world— rather, view it as an opportunity  to learn how to improve and adapt in preparation for your next attempt. Viewing failure as a stepping stone to a successful conclusion tends to trigger your positive mindset to kick in.

- If you have an idea for a project or a goal, but never start it, or you abandon it halfway through, you could later have feelings of regret. The more important the project or goal, the greater the feelings of regret will probably be.

- Some of us are afraid to be criticized or judged for failing. The solution to this is to realize that those who truly care about you will not criticize you. In fact, quite the opposite—those people who matter in your life will encourage you to make another attempt. Equally important is to bear in mind that there are those who get joy out of seeing others fail. Don't bother with these kinds of people.

- Being a perfectionist can cause you to fail. Perfectionists believe that to succeed they must produce perfect results every time. Because of this, they sometimes won't even make a start, or they will give up a project midway. See Chapter 25 - You Don't Have to Be Perfect.

- There are times when someone will offer you an opportunity or you will decide to develop a project of your own. Next thing you know, you are overwhelmed by intimidating thoughts coming from your inner critic. Your inner critic is that voice inside your head telling you that you haven't got what it takes to succeed or that you will fail or look foolish, or worse, all of the above.

Many times, what the inner critic is telling you goes back to something that occurred or was told to you in your childhood years, though I know of cases where the origins occurred post-childhood.

In one-on-one sessions, a competent professional can resolve the "inner critic" issue by dealing with where, when, and how it originated.

For now, counteract the voice of your inner critic, which rarely tells the truth or exaggerates, by minimizing it. Many have found that an effective way of minimizing the critic is to give it a comical voice.

- Don't hesitate or feel shy about asking for advice.

- Amaze yourself: go out there and do something you thought you couldn't do. Even if you don't succeed, giving it your best effort is enough to feel good about! In addition, the experience and new knowledge you acquire from the attempt will always benefit you.

- Start by setting small goals to help build your confidence. Once you have achieved those goals, make the next set of goals a little more challenging. By gradually but deliberately moving forward, you will begin to overcome your fear of failure.

- As you move forward with your desire to overcome your fear of failure, be sure to show yourself the same patience that you would show to someone you care about.

Use the power of your imagination:

1. Choose your goal. It must be specific with a reasonable completion time. Your goal must also be believable and attainable—wanting to climb Mt. Everest by the middle of next week is hardly a believable or attainable goal.

2. Read the following four steps and then practice the technique.

3. Close your eyes, take a deep breath and visualize yourself on the path to success.

4. If you see yourself 'failing' or 'falling' along your path, visualize or imagine yourself confidently making the necessary adjustments to succeed. Now see yourself looking determined and energized continuing towards your target.

5. See a bright and colorful picture of yourself succeeding, and, if you choose to, add sound effects. Simultaneously, feel the feeling of what it will be like to succeed.

6. Turn up the volume and increase the brightness of the image of the successful you. Feel the satisfying feeling of completion and success throughout your entire body, from the top of your head to the tips of your toes.

Repeat this technique at least twice a day. Successful business people and athletes use this same technique, it works for them—with practice let it work for you!

The moment failure consents to adjustment, it begins to take on the robes of upcoming success.

Chapter 27

It's Okay to Say "No"

"I cannot give the formula for success, but I can give the formula for failure—try to please everybody."

Herbert B. Swope

Saying "no" at the appropriate time is a very positive act. Saying "no" clearly does not mean that you are being rude, uncaring or that you want to sever connections with those around you. Saying "no" can be positively applied to family and work situations, and to many other aspects of life. There are no hard and fast rules to saying "no." Say "no" when you feel it is appropriate.

The benefits of saying "no":

- In your dealings with family and friends, there are times when, in the interest of having more favorable outcomes, that it is best to say "no." This holds very true in parenting as well.

- Saying "no" allows you to give your full and undivided attention to your current projects and commitments.

- Always saying "yes" can have a detrimental effect on your health. It can give rise to stress and drain your energy when you take on too much. That stress often manifests as exhaustion, skin breakouts, high blood pressure or other physical and mental symptoms. See Chapter 28 on taking good care of yourself.

- Be sure to remember that you are not a plug-in machine designed to function 24/7. By attempting to please all of the people all of the time, you are asking too much of yourself. You may want to help others, but if you take on too much at one time, your own ship starts sinking and you are no longer in a position to help those around you.

- It is okay to say "no" to the people who continually ask for your help, when they are quite capable of helping themselves. For those who don't know how to do the job and are capable of learning how to do it, then your teaching them how will result in two winners—they will learn to achieve some independence and you will have more time for yourself.

- Saying "yes" to avoid conflict is rarely a good solution. In some cases, by saying yes, you are unintentionally "training" certain people to take advantage of you and this is clearly not a good thing. When you do decide to say "no" to people, they will have more respect for you and your time. This, in turn, will increase your own sense of worth.

Saying "no" when you feel it is appropriate helps you take control of your life.

The ways to say "no":

- Be polite and courteous. Once you have said "no," decide whether there is a need to offer an explanation. If you choose to explain, most people will accept and respect a well-reasoned decision.

- Simply say that you are unable to take on additional work or duties at the present time.

- Say that you are so sorry, but that you will not be able to give the request all the attention it deserves.

Adopting a new behavior like saying "no," can be a little challenging at first. Simply say "no" once and then feel and appreciate the benefit of your action. Saying "no" will become easier and easier.

Give yourself a big "YES" for beginning to say "NO" .

Chapter 28

Take Good Care Of Yourself

"If you must love your neighbor as yourself, it is at least fair to love yourself as you do your neighbor."

Nicholas De Chamfort

Many of us spend much of our time attending to the well-being of family and friends without pausing to take into account our own energy levels and state of well-being. This results in negative impacts on ourselves.

The following scenario illustrates how we can better take care of others when we are in good shape; a badly-wounded soldier needs to be carried 200 yards by one of his platoon members to a waiting helicopter that will transport him to a military hospital for emergency surgery.

Not far from the severely wounded soldier is a moderately wounded soldier who, despite his injuries, makes a courageous attempt to carry his comrade to the helicopter but, because of his injuries, he is not in good enough shape to do so. Fortunately a third soldier at a further distance, but with no injuries, is able to run over and carry the badly-wounded soldier to the helicopter.

The point here: You must be in the best shape possible in order to help others, so you must ensure that you are taking good care of yourself.

Here are some proven suggestions:

- You cannot please all the people all the time and doing so will ultimately wear you down. See Chapter 27 - It's OK to Say "No".

- Sleep and relaxation are vitally important—make sure you are getting enough of both. Most parents are aware that when their young children are exhausted and have been overwhelmed with too much activity they could become prone to having a temper tantrum. We adults often don't notice when exhaustion creeps up on us but, when it does, it can also result in emotional breakdown, rendering us temporarily unfit to perform our tasks.

- Have regular medical check-ups, eat healthy and exercise.

- Practice mindfulness to increase your tranquility. **As a bonus your tranquility can have a calming effect on those around you, making you an agent for positive change.** See Chapter 57 – Mindful Methods in Minutes.

- Occasionally go out and spoil yourself.

Chapter 29

Shield Yourself

"Do what you can, with what you have, where you are."

Theodore Roosevelt

Ever find yourself in a situation where certain family members or work associates have the annoying and hurtful habit of throwing negative comments at you?

Suggestions to protect yourself:

- Ask those people to kindly cease their behavior and see what happens. Perhaps one or more of them don't quite realize the negative effects of their actions.

- Carefully consider your own actions to ensure that you intentionally or unintentionally are not the not the cause of the problem. It could be most constructive to actually ask the other party what it is you might be doing to offend them.

- Bear in mind that the darts they are throwing might be a manifestation of their own insecurities and inadequacies, and if you were not the target, they would probably find someone else to attack.

Here is a useful technique to help you protect yourself from being struck by their verbal darts:

Instant Shield Technique

1. Close your eyes, and then rapidly create an

impenetrable shield all around you. This shield, can be made of any material, and be of any color you choose.

2. Next time anyone starts throwing those darts at you, immediately surround yourself with your shield.

Instant
Protective Shield!

3. Imagine hearing the sound of their negative words hitting your shield, and then hear them falling harmlessly onto the floor.

If you are going to be walking into a space and have a strong feeling that the darts will fly, surround yourself with your shield before entering.

The more you practice this technique, the more protective your shield becomes.

Chapter 30

Replenish Your Energy

"I must choose between despair and energy—I choose the latter."
                                                    John Keats

When you are caught completely off guard by a family member, someone at work or anyone else who suddenly verbally attacks you, it can feel as if some of your energy has been sucked right out of you. You might even experience it as a blow to your stomach. Here's a way to rapidly replenish your energy.

Energy Replenishment Technique
Read and remember the following three steps. Use the technique when required.

1. Close your eyes and then scan your body and notice any holes or gaps where your energy has been partially or completely sucked out of you.

2. Imagine, sense or feel new positive energy moving into and filling all those holes and gaps. The replacement

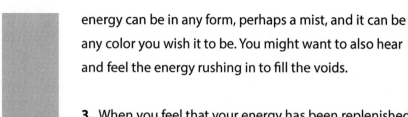

energy can be in any form, perhaps a mist, and it can be any color you wish it to be. You might want to also hear and feel the energy rushing in to fill the voids.

3. When you feel that your energy has been replenished, slowly open your eyes and continue with your day, feeling refreshed, revitalized and ready to go on!

Chapter 31

A Good Night's Sleep

"Sleep is that golden chain that ties health and our bodies together."
Thomas Dekker

There is no doubt about the importance of a good night's sleep. Without sleep, it is difficult to live each day as we would like. The following is a list of well-tested suggestions to help you get the sleep you need to function efficiently:

- Your bedroom is the place where you sleep. Remove TVs, computers, and all electronic equipment (except medical equipment) from your bedroom. Remove everything related to your work, and do not eat in your bedroom. If you want to sleep well, it is vitally important that your subconscious mind knows that your bedroom is not an electronic entertainment area, a dining room, or a workspace, but that it is only known as the place where you sleep. Although these changes may be a little difficult to get used to, consider the reward of a good night's sleep.

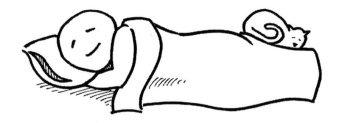

- Don't nap during the day. Save your sleep for later.
- Fresh air and exercise contribute to better sleep. In addition, they

also improve your emotional and physical well-being.

- Caffeine will keep you up, while alcohol often produces a shallow, unrestful type of sleep. Make an effort to limit both.

Tomorrow's Plan Technique
If you tend to wake in the middle of the night and can't immediately go back to sleep because your mind is active and concerned with all the things you have to do tomorrow, do the following:

Before you retire for the night, take a sheet of paper and draw a line down the center. On one side of the line, list all of tomorrow's tasks. On the other side, write down how you are going to take care of each one. If you wake up thinking or worrying about a task, reach over to your night table, pick up the list, read it and then say "back to sleep, I have a plan and I know exactly what to do."

- Use any of the relaxation techniques printed in this book, both before you go to sleep and if you wake up during the night.

- Begin winding down about an hour before you go to bed.

- Take a warm bath or shower before bedtime.

- Before turning off the light, recall all the good things that happened to you during the day.

- If your muscles are feeling tensed up, do the Progressive Muscle Relaxer found in Chapter 8.

- Close your eyes and 'see' or imagine whatever mental images you find to be restful and sleep-inducing.

Technique of Opposite Intentions

If you are forcing yourself to fall asleep but it's just not working, then instead of becoming upset and frustrated, **do the exact opposite—do your utmost to stay awake for as long as you can.** Instead of thinking "I must go to sleep right now," change your thinking to "I must do whatever it takes to stay awake. I must make sure that my eyes don't close, I cannot allow them to close." The more you lie still and consciously keep your eyes open, the more difficult it is to stay awake.

Chapter 32

Mindful Eating And Slimming

"It is better to eat to live, than to live to eat."

Jean Moliere

Mindful eating is a beneficial habit. It can have a strong effect on limiting how much you eat. Even if you are not actively engaged in reducing weight, mindful eating can make a significant difference to your eating experience and food digestion.

Today, we often just chow down our food without paying enough attention to the food's unique flavors, textures and aromas. We tend to swallow our food so rapidly that by the time the brain receives a message from the nerve endings in the stomach saying it is full, we have already swallowed another unnecessary mouthful or two.

To combat this unhealthy eating style, consider practicing the following mindful eating habits:

- Always eat sitting down.

- Before you eat, a brief affirmation of gratitude or a few moments of silence alerts your mind that you are about to eat with the intention of refueling your body.

- Drink a glass of water before you eat. It will reduce the temptation to wolf down your food.

- Eat specific portions of healthy food. A nutritionist, dietitian or your doctor can best advise which particular foods and portion sizes are suitable for you.

- Use smaller plates. The same-size serving on a smaller plate appears bigger and more filling than when it is placed on a larger plate. On a larger plate it looks little, lost and not enough. We do tend to eat with our eyes!

Little and Lost   Full and Filling

- Serve up in the kitchen. Serving bowls on the dining table are a temptation for more helpings.

- Once you have served the food, immediately place the remainder in storage containers and stow them away in the fridge. This strategy makes going for second helpings more of an effort!

- Place only bite-size portions in your mouth at a time.

- Before you start chewing, place your knife and fork on your plate. Our minds are only capable of fully concentrating on one activity at a time. If your mind is going to divert its attention to the activity of holding the cutlery, then it will be unable to fully focus on the fact that you are eating and fueling your body.

- The "fun of food" is in your mouth, to increase the fun and enjoyment of your food, chew it consciously, slowly and deliberately, and while you do that, become aware of every flavor and texture. Before long, you will become a "food artist" who appreciates every morsel. There is an added bonus to deliberately and mindfully chewing each mouthful of food—it brings you into The Now.

- Chew your food until it is a paste and then, and only then, swallow it. This process will also make for easier digestion.

- The moment you feel full, do not eat what remains on your plate. Immediately discard the leftovers or store them for another day. Leaving nothing on the plate entitles one to be a member of The Clean Plate Club. What is notable about this club is that it has absolutely no benefits at all.

- At the end of the meal, stay at the table for two quiet minutes. These two important minutes, will allow your mind the time it needs to acknowledge that your stomach has been filled. A sand-filled egg timer is perfect for measuring the two minutes.

- Whenever you go to a restaurant, ask the waiter to bring a take-out container to the table at the same time he brings your order. When the food arrives, immediately divide your meal into two halves and place one half in the take-out container. Hand the container to your waiter and have him give it back to you when you depart. Two good things come out of this: you only eat what your body requires, and you don't have to prepare your next meal.

- Most of us are subject to food cravings. There is a noticeable difference between food cravings and hunger. Food cravings grow fast, while hunger takes several hours to build up. The moment a craving pops up, ward it off by having a glass of water, changing your physical location, stepping outside for a brief walk, or creating another diversion. Another effective technique to deal with a craving is to re-place it with the certain knowledge that it will subside. Practice doing one of these and your temptation to satisfy the craving will decrease.

- **Never eat while watching TV or talking on the phone.** These particular habits prevent you from being aware of all the excess food you are unconsciously dumping into your body. Take care and be selective of what and how much you eat. If you do not take care of your car, it will break down on the highway. Your body is no different.

- When eating food directly from a bag, you are unable to see how much you are really eating; it's easy to eat much more than you need, even if the food is healthy. A simple solution to stop eating this way is to place the right amount of food on a plate and stow the rest of the bag away.

- Once you have eaten and are tempted to eat more, counteract the temptation by thinking or saying the words: "This excess food will soon become more of me."

- Go one step further by actually imagining yourself walking around with that excess food—pastries, chicken wings smothered in sauce, or slices of heavily-topped pizza—permanently stuck to the outside of your clothing!

- When tempted to eat that cookie or something similar, say to yourself: "I will get a quick 20 seconds of pleasure, but I will also be jeopardizing my future."

- A really powerful technique is to close your eyes and visualize or imagine yourself at your desired weight. Make that picture of yourself as bright and happy as you can. While doing so, visualize yourself practicing mindful eating and doing whatever else you have chosen to do to reach your desired weight. Feel throughout your body, from the top of your head down to the tips of your toes, the good feeling you associate with having successfully slimmed down to your desired weight. Now, intensify the visual and the feeling. This technique, like all other visualization techniques, becomes more effective the more you repeat it and the more passion and feeling you put into it.

Chapter 33

Be a Mover

"Lack of activity destroys the good condition of every human being, while movement and physical exercise save it and preserve it."   *Plato*

When we exercise, signals from the brain trigger the production of the biochemicals and hormones that have a positive effect on our mood, energy and all round health.

We all know and acknowledge the mental and physical benefits of exercising, but for most of us, exercising can be a challenge that is easier said than done. We could well do with ideas and suggestions to get us going.

When you decide to start moving, the following suggestions will help motivate you:

- Write down how moving your body will benefit you. Read this list at least twice a day.

- Make your moving routine specific and manageable.

- Avoid elevators and escalators when possible, take the stairs instead.

- Park far away from your destination on purpose.

- Yoga is an excellent form of exercise both for the body and the mind. There are various types of yoga. Find the one that is most suited to your needs.

- Activities like dance classes, hiking, skating and team sports get you moving. Besides being healthy and fun, activities like these allow for social connectivity—maybe with family members or new friends who also want to become movers.

- There are many events that rely on walkers and runners to raise funds for good causes. These events are great opportunities to introduce yourself into a moving routine.

- Know that you don't have to love exercise, but it's best that you do it. Many people start out not exactly loving it, but with time they find it gives them satisfaction.

- If you find exercising boring, listen to motivating and energizing music or some other audio entertainment to help the time pass.

- Place your walking shoes near the front door. They will be your reminder.

- If possible, find someone to move with. This motivates you, and makes you both accountable to each other.

- Tell your friends and family that you are going to exercise. This, too, will hold you accountable and keep you motivated.

- If on a particular day you are pressed for time or just don't feel like moving your body, tell yourself that you will do half of your usual amount of moving. Once you have started, chances are you will be into it and want to keep going.

- The more you visualize or imagine yourself becoming fitter and fitter, the more your subconscious mind will help motivate you to do what it takes to accomplish your goals.

Exercising or moving reduces some of the effects of stress:

Exercising plays an important role in the release of the "feel good" hormone, serotonin. It also reduces some of the physical effects of stress by helping release muscle tension often felt in neck and shoulder areas.

Back when we were hunters and gatherers a surprise encounter with a saber-tooth tiger caused us to fight or flee. To fire up the fight-or-flight response, the adrenal gland spewed the stress hormone, cortisol, into the body. The resulting high level of cortisol was soon reduced by the physical activity of fighting or fleeing.

The fears and stresses that confront us today are the saber-tooth tigers of modern day living. They have the same physiological effects on us as the saber-tooth tigers had on our ancestors. Since our world is much more stressful than theirs was, we have more instances of cortisol flowing into our bodies. An accumulation of cortisol is a threat to our well-being and can also cause a breakdown of the immune system, making us more prone to illness.

A sedentary lifestyle is not conducive to lowering cortisol levels, but regular physical activity helps. Your activity needn't be a specific sport or exercise; refer to the "moving" methods and suggestions mentioned in this chapter. You don't have to become the next Olympic gold medalist; just move to keep your self in healthy shape.

(You might want to read the works of Canadian biochemist, Hans Selye, a pioneering expert on this subject).

Caution: Before starting a new exercise routine, consult your doctor, especially if you have current or previous respiratory or cardiac issues.

Chapter 34

"I Can"

"If you hear a voice within you say "you cannot paint," then by all means paint, and that voice will soon be silenced."

Vincent van Gogh

When we face challenges, there are times when we tend to shy away from them. One way this negative tendency can be overcome is by taking notice of the accomplishments of those who have faced greater challenges than us. Many of those brave and courageous people might not have all their limbs or faculties, yet they have managed to do much of what most of us take for granted. For example, some learned to paint, play instruments, participate in sports, drive cars, and once again get on with life. Their "I can" mindset played a vital role in helping them to achieve against the odds. These people are fine examples and inspirations to all of us and, in recognition of them, I sum it up this way:

"Because They Can"
Because against the odds they can,
Then, with all my faculties I can,
And if I can,
Then you can,
And if you and I can,
Then we all can!
And when you feel you can't,
Hear them say: "I can."

Question Technique

When you are confronted with a situation that appears difficult to manage, self-limiting statements like, "I can't do this" or "I give up, it's too difficult," will prevent you from moving forward.

A constructive alternative is to change your self-limiting statements into questions:

- "I can't do this" becomes "How can I figure out how to do this?"

- "I give up; this is too difficult" becomes "What makes this so difficult?"

This questioning mindset readily allows you to search for solutions and promote a positive attitude for achievement.

When you are faced with a challenge, whatever its size, and however daunting it may seem, let those who have achieved under difficult circumstances be your role models and inspiration. Allow those two powerful words—**I CAN**—to propel you to your accomplishment.

Instead of giving yourself reasons why you can't, give yourself reasons why you can.

> This chapter is dedicated to wounded servicemen and service-women, challenged athletes and all those with disabilities and to all the caring organizations and volunteers. You are each, in your own unique way, a source of inspiration. Your attitude and achievements beam to all around you the power of "I Can."

Chapter 35

Changing Habits and Behaviors

"Human beings, by changing the inner attitudes of their minds, can change the outer aspects of their lives."

William James

Habits arise because of a desire to fill or satisfy a need. Nail-biters bite their nails because they find it to be a way of coping with anxiety or some other issue. Many smokers started smoking at a very young age in order to be accepted by their peers. These actions, which once started as being "beneficial," have now become bad habits that are difficult to break (even though we may consciously know that they are bad for us).

To stop a habit, the reasons for stopping MUST be stronger than the reasons for continuing. For help in making the decision whether to stop a bad habit, or not, draw a vertical line down the center of a sheet of paper. On one side of the line, write down all the reasons to continue the bad habit. On the other side of the line, write down all the benefits of stopping. Carefully consider the pros and cons and decide what is going to be best for you. On the con side make doubly sure you have included the long-term negative effects of continuing the habit. Changing habits and behaviors, just like other similar situations in life, do not happen overnight, but with consistent effort favorable results are possible.

Here are techniques to overcome habits:

Substitute Technique

To help overcome a habit, substitute the negative habit with a more positive stand-in that is healthier or less destructive. Instead of biting their nails, nail-biters can hold and move small objects around in their hand (coins work well). Smokers can place a plastic coffee stirrer between their lips instead of lighting up. Using a little creativity, it is easy to come up with alternatives to any habit.

Sweep Technique

1. First read through all of the following steps.

2. Close your eyes and visualize or imagine a poster or a painting showing the specific results and consequences

of your particular bad habit. For example, it could be you at your current weight, or with bitten nails, or lungs coated with greasy, toxic chemicals.

3. Now, fade the particular image that applies to your bad habit to a dull gray, just as if it were a faded or old photograph.

4. Shrink the size of this faded image, or if you prefer, you can "push" it out into the distance, where it also becomes smaller and less distinct.

5. Visualize or imagine a bright and colorful image of yourself looking slimmer after having taken the appropriate measures to reduce your weight. Nail-biters can create an image of their hands with healthy and attractive nails, while smokers can visualize clean lungs or a vibrant and healthy picture of themselves. You can create any image that works for you, as long as it clearly shows the beneficial results of having stopped your particular bad habit.

6. Make the successful "after" image bigger, more colorful, and brighter.

7. Now this is the "Sweep" step, so-called because it provides you with the opportunity to sweep away unwanted habits and make your changes. Close your eyes and visualize the smaller faded "before" image; then completely cover it over with the larger, more colorful and brighter "after" image. While you cover-over, say, with total conviction, the word: "Sweep." The more emotion and conviction you express while verbalizing this affirmation, the more powerful the technique becomes, and the quicker and greater its effect. While saying the word "Sweep," you can increase its force by making a sweeping motion with your arm across your upper body.

8. After completing each "cover-over," open your eyes, then look up for a second, look down for a second, look to your left for a second, look to your right for a second. This is called the break state and is an integral part of the process.

Repeat the "cover-over" process 10 times. Do the first three "cover-overs" slowly, and then increasingly speed up the remaining seven.

Do 10 sets of the "Sweep" technique twice a day, or more if you want. Do it for at least 30 days. Two or three minutes is all that's needed to do a set of 10 "Sweep" cover-overs. By consistently practicing this process, you imprint a new and positive change into your subconscious mind.

Countering Habits With Relaxation

The desire to stop performing the bad habits associated with stress or anxiety can be achieved by diligently practicing relaxation and mindfulness techniques, many of which are found in this book. A tranquil and relaxed state is an excellent counter-measure to the performance of these habits. See the quick relaxation techniques in Chapter 7 and the mindfulness methods in Chapter 57.

Note: It is important to note that habits become weaker the longer you do not perform them.

You Be The Change Technique

Mahatma Gandhi, the renowned philosopher and political change-maker, wisely stated that a person could make a change by becoming the change. If, for example, you want to make the change to become more confident, then first select a person who has the confident traits and qualities that you would like for yourself. Walk the way that person walks, imitate as closely as you can their facial expressions, talk the way they would talk, and so forth. By doing so, you effectively become the change. Please note that by making a change it does not imply that you are a phony or a pretender. It's simply you being in control, making a decision and exercising your right to make the changes that you want for yourself.

Due to the neuroplasticity of the brain, your new thoughts and actions contribute to creating new and more efficient neural pathways which, after a while, will cause the newly chosen behaviors to feel increasingly more natural. For more details on changing thoughts and behaviors, see Chapter 4 - Thoughts and Feelings.

**It's never too late to be habit- free—
nor the person you want to be.**

Chapter 36

Perseverance Wins

"Perseverance is a great element of success. If you only knock long and loud enough at the gate, you are sure to wake up somebody."
Henry W. Longfellow

Techniques to enhance perseverance:

Take yourself into your perseverance zone:

1. Close your eyes, and visualize or imagine yourself persevering at your task, goal or project.

2. Let yourself go further into your perseverance zone; don't force it, just let it happen and be there.See and feel your perseverance taking you to your achievements and success.

3. Increase the feeling and intensity of being in your perseverance zone by making the image you see or imagine stronger and brighter, and by turning up the good feelings you associate with your succeeding. Do this quick exercise at least 2 or 3 times a day.

Visualizing and imagining are super-powerful tools. Use them – they are your weapons for success.

When the going gets tough and you are thinking about giving up, restore your sense of purpose and enthusiasm by recalling, remembering and re-experiencing your "in the perseverance zone" visualization and the positive feeling it gave you.

Perseverance Road

Model yourself on, and adopt the ways of, the many role models who struggled up "Perseverance Road" before anything significant happened to them.

On the way to your own success be prepared to walk a distance up "Perseverance Road." It's a tough road with little compromise. Some days and nights your walk could be all uphill and on others it might be in the cold and pouring rain. Many famous and successful people had that struggle. They hung in and kept pushing forward. The following are true-life examples of those who kept at it, swept their disappointments aside and focused on conquering the grueling grind.

- **The Beatles,** and a long list of musicians, actors and artists, were initially rejected by recording studios, movie studios and art galleries. It took effort and time before they were offered contracts and received the well-deserved fruits of their perseverance.
- **Thomas Edison**, in his quest to invent new products, had one failure after another but he would not be discouraged. Besides giving us the electric light bulb, Edison developed many devices that greatly influenced life around the world. His constant perseverance paid off.
- **J.K. Rowling**, creator of the Harry Potter series, was turned down by one publisher after another, but she pushed on undeterred. Nothing was going to stop her until she succeeded.

There are many other people who succeeded because of their unwavering perseverance. Follow their leads, do what they did, and keep on driving forward.

Never Ever Quit. Your success could be just around the next corner!

Here is another useful tip:

Super-charge your journey to success by combining Perseverance with the two other P's.

1. **Picturing** (visualizing) the project.

2. Devoting your **Passion** to the project.

3. Applying your **Perseverance** to the project.

The combination of Picturing, Passion and Perseverance produces a powerful potion for success: "3P" The Potent Success Potion.

Put your success in motion. Partake of the potion.

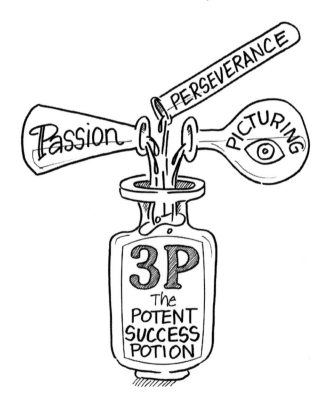

Chapter 37

Business Success and Motivation

"Whatever you can do, or dream you can—begin it. Boldness has genius, power, and magic in it."   *J.W. Goethe*

The reason I have included this chapter is because business success, at any level, provides many people with a source of happiness and satisfaction.

There is seldom a quick and easy way for any worthwhile business venture to succeed. Growing a business is not a quick dash or even a sprint; it's a marathon.

Time-tested methods to help achieve success:

- It is absolutely imperative to have a well-thought-out and deeply-researched business plan with a definite direction to follow. If you do not follow your plan closely enough, or if you decide to take too many short cuts, you may find yourself losing your way and you could arrive at the wrong destination.

- Do not conduct your market research on family and friends. Often they will tell you what you want to hear. It is vitally important to step out of your home or office and present your product or service to the actual people who will have to pay to acquire it.

- When exposing your product to the market, listen and take note of all the comments and feedback you might hear. Make the appropriate adjustments to make your product more sellable.

- Never take any comments about your product personally. You and your product are two totally separate entities. The moment you allow your emotions or feelings of hurt to take over, step back to reassess. Ask yourself which of the two is more important, your ego or the success of your business?

- If possible, work with a mentor. Besides providing you with invaluable advice, a mentor could fast-track your venture by introducing you to opportunities and connecting you to the right people.

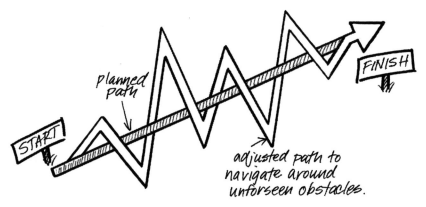

- Make a point of regularly monitoring your progress. Make the necessary adjustments when needed and navigate around unforeseen obstacles as they arise.

- Get out of your comfort zone and go that extra mile. Passion and sacrifice are vital to the success of every venture!

- Take good care of your customers or clients, without them you don't have a business or a source for referrals.

- Seek advice from experts. It's pointless making errors or incurring unnecessary expenses when advice is available to you.

- Harness the power of your mind. If you imagine failure, then you are unlikely to succeed. However, if you visualize your success and have determined "I can and will" thoughts, then your chance of succeeding is more likely to increase. See Chapter 4 - Thoughts and Feelings, on the development of positive neural pathways.

- Don't be rushed or stampeded into making important decisions. In almost all circumstances, it is acceptable and reasonable to inform the other party that you want more time to think through the matter and that you will get back to them as soon as you can.

- Always bear in mind that almost everything is negotiable. When you are purchasing goods or services for your business, wear your negotiator's cap and work out a deal that is best for you. Don't start the negotiations by informing the vendor what you are prepared to pay; that's "showing your cards." Rather, allow the vendor to give his price first, then negotiate to a price that betters or meets your budget. Quantity discounts and payment terms are also important subjects for negotiation. If the dollar amount is significant enough, call more than one vendor for comparative bids.

- Ignore those who say "It will never work." If it doesn't work, you can always make adjustments and start again. It often takes a measure of trial and error to attain success.

- Operate and run your business with a sense of urgency. With a "gotta get it done now" mindset you will achieve more in less time. Your sense of urgency will also continually set a standard for your employees, positively influencing their overall performance. Most businesses have stiff competition; so move ahead rapidly and see your opposition in your rear view mirror! Return emails and phone calls related to sales inquiries as soon as you can. Too many sales opportunities are lost because the replies did not go out fast enough.

- When pitching your product or service to a store or organization, or for that matter to any potential customer, make doubly sure, right from the very start, that you are speaking to the right person. Anything less than dealing directly with the buyer or decision maker, will, in all likelihood, be a waste of your time and energy. I can't stress this strongly enough.

- If you make any agreements or contracts with other parties, its best to get them in writing.

- Join business networking groups in your area. They are useful vehicles to grow your business. They also offer opportunities to become involved in the greater community.

Chapter 38

Worries, Fears And Catastrophic Thoughts

"How much pain they have caused us, the evils that never happened."
Thomas Jefferson

Some of us spend too big a portion of our days and nights worrying and having fearful thoughts. This causes unnecessary mental anguish, and because of the mind-body connection, it can also cause physical suffering and pain.

The more you think about your worries and fears, the larger they become, even to where they become debilitating. Our worries, fears and catastrophic thoughts are often illogical and not an accurate interpretation of the actual facts. They can grow and intensify in our minds to the point where they take on a life of their own, and next thing they begin to rule us.

There are ways to deal with these overwhelming fears and worries:

- **Challenge their validity.** Sit down in a quiet place and analyze what is causing your fears and worries. You will often find that, although they appear real, they are not based in reality, and that the evidence to support them is false.

    F-E-A-R = False Evidence Appearing Real

- List your fears and worries, and then let a trusted friend or associate give you his viewpoint. Listen quietly. Often your friend's objective view will help you realize that there is nothing to worry about.

- Never worry alone. Share your worry with a friend or family, but at times the best person to share with is a professional who is expert in this area.

- Calmly approach your worry or fear. Often the closer you get to it, the more you will notice that the ferocious bull you thought it was is just a gentle calf.

- Stop catastrophic thoughts from escalating by calming yourself down with, for example, the 18 Second Relaxer in Chapter 7. When you are in a calm frame of mind, it is so much easier to see everything in its true perspective.

- **With most of life's events, there is a big difference between what's possibly going to happen and what's probably going to happen.** Anything is possible. It's possible that there will be an earthquake in the next 30 seconds, but it is not probable that this will happen. Expose your catastrophic thoughts about possible future events to the same logic and your fears will subside.

- **Don't spend time "what-iffing."** What if this terrible event happens and what if that unpleasant event happens? "What if my employer decides to relocate to another city?" "What if my son doesn't get into the college of his choice?" "What if my loan application is not approved?"

One can choose to "what-if" until the end of time, or choose to get on with life and deal with a situation only once it arises. If the situation does turn out to be challenging, you will be pleasantly surprised by your resilience and ability to make it through.

- Ask yourself if in the past you have ever had similar catastrophic thoughts about the same issue you are facing now. If the answer is yes, ask yourself how everything turned out the last time. If everything turned out fine then, it will most likely turn out fine again.

- Some people endlessly churn over and re-examine their problems and issues non-stop. They do this believing that they will eventually gain a clear understanding of who they really are and how to overcome all of their obstacles. On the contrary, they achieve very little benefits. What they do acquire are more truckloads of increased pessimism, gloom and sadness. If churning and re-examining is not improving your situation, talk to the right set of ears to short-cut the path to reaching practical, real-world solutions.

- Imagine a friend has approached you with their worries, fears and catastrophic thoughts; what would you tell them? This exercise will allow you to see things from another perspective and, if positive and appropriate, you might consider adapting and applying your responses to yourself.

Chapter 39

Control Racing and Obsessive Thoughts

"To the mind that is still, the whole universe surrenders."

Lao Tzu

There are times when our minds are filled with racing or obsessive thoughts, both of which make us anxious and fearful. These thoughts are disruptive and tend to wear us down.

Here are techniques to help you:

Stop at Stop Signs Technique

Close your eyes and imagine a red and white STOP sign right in front of you. Now think of the danger of going through a STOP sign. The next time the racing thoughts start, visualize the STOP sign right in front of you. Every time you do this, you are increasing your thought control and training your brain to interrupt the racing thought pattern. You can draw a stop sign on the palm of your hand and when the racing thoughts start going, stop them by looking at your palm.

Distraction Technique

Distract yourself from racing and obsessive thoughts by turning on the radio and listening to a talk show on low volume. Because the volume is low, you have to listen intently. This creates a diversion from your thoughts. Engage in enjoyable or interesting activities. They could include ,gardening, card games, arts and crafts, learning to play a musical instrument or whatever keeps your mind entertained and occupied.

V-e-r-y S-l-o-w-l-y Technique

Pause and say each and every word of the racing thoughts v-e-r-y s-l-o-w-l-y. By doing this, you will not only take back control of the speed of your thoughts, you will also gain the opportunity to analyze each one of them. Analyzing your thoughts gives you the chance to separate the important ones from the irrelevant ones.

Zen-Way Technique

Place your tongue in contact with the roof of your mouth. Slowly inhale and exhale through your nose until the thoughts slow down or stop. This technique is rooted in Zen culture.

Cartoonize Technique

Reduce the power of obsessive thoughts by giving them a silly sound track. Give the thoughts comical voices. Some of my clients have "cartoonized" their obsessive thoughts or imagined them in ridiculous-looking costumes and found this has worked for them. Use your imagination and enjoy the resulting relief!

Sing-a-Silly-Song Technique

An adaption of the previous technique is to recall a silly song. If you don't have one, find one on the Internet. Whenever the obsessive thoughts come into your mind, start singing the silly song either silently or out loud.

Exercise, beneficial as it is for both for mind and body, can play a role in reducing racing and obsessive thoughts. The endorphins produced in the brain when exercising promote a feeling of well-being. When we are enjoying a feeling of well-being, we are in a better frame of mind to control and take charge of these disruptive thoughts.

When the body's muscles are relaxed, this too can contribute to a general feeling of well-being and less stresses on the mind. See Chapter 8-Progressive Muscle Relaxer.

Chapter 40

Throw Out Self-doubt and Negative Thoughts

"Our doubts are traitors, and make us lose the good we often might win, by fearing to attempt."　　　*William Shakespeare*

First let's find out how negative thoughts and self-doubts become imprinted in our minds. After that, we'll explore a way to stop them. Having negative thoughts about yourself is never productive. Even worse, by repeating these negative thoughts over and over again, they become deeply imprinted into your subconscious mind. Soon these negative thoughts become the facts that you believe to be the truth about who you are. They start to define you. This will have a damaging effect on your self-esteem.

Question: How do these negative thoughts imprint and amplify?
Answer: If I ask you what is 4 x 5, you would probably automatically give the correct answer. This is because your math teacher, by constant repetition, imprinted the times tables into your subconscious mind. In the same way, negative self-thoughts are also imprinted into our subconscious minds.

Each time you think something negative about yourself, a threefold amplification of the negative thought occurs in the following way:
1. You make the **first imprint** in your subconscious mind when you **think** the negative thought.
2. You make the **second imprint** when you **say** the

negative thought.

3. You make the **third imprint** when you **hear** what you have said.

Part or all of this sequence produces imprints and confirmations of the negative thoughts you have of yourself. Now consider how deeply imprinted the negative thought will become when you repeat part or all of this sequence **several times** a day. No part of this helps you feel good about yourself, nor does it help you become successful, so it's best to take steps to avoid negative thoughts in the first place.

Boldly question and challenge your self-doubts. You are often far more capable than you believe you are.

There are times when you want to move forward or accomplish something but find that you are stuck. You are inhibited or even paralyzed by your self-doubts, and as a consequence, you miss out on many of the opportunities of life. In addition, self-doubt has very negative effects on your self-confidence.

The Courtroom of The Mind Technique helps throw out self-doubts and negative thoughts:
Most of us do not take the time to ponder or analyze the validity of our negative self-thoughts. We become so accepting of them and as time goes by the thoughts take up permanent residency in our minds. This technique, applied correctly, can be very effective. Use it—you be

the judge and jury and THROW YOUR SELF-DOUBTS OUT OF COURT!

In the illustration, the self-doubt in this particular case is the doubt of being able to do a particular task. Visualize or imagine what is happening in the courtroom. To really make the scene come alive, take on the roles of all the participants. (Follow the numbers in the picture 1-4.)

The moment you have a self-doubt or a negative thought, create a court room in your mind and then follow the procedure as shown or insert your own words. **Throw out the self-doubt and boldly move forward and do whatever it is you choose to do; no more self-doubts, nothing holding you back!**

Chapter 41

Exit Your House of Pain

"You cannot prevent the birds of sadness from passing over your head, but you can prevent them from nesting in your hair." *Swedish Proverb*

There are times in our lives when current or recent events cause us to feel that everything is crashing around us and simultaneously collapsing within us; so much so, that we become despondent and withdraw into what becomes our "house of pain." We could find ourselves in this house because of a broken relationship, a business venture that suddenly collapsed, a breakdown in the family; the list goes on. We lock the doors and shutter the windows. There is a deep dark around us and an even deeper dark within us.

Our pain increases and our confidence crumbles. Increasingly we identify as victims. But, just because something emotionally unpleasant happened, there is really no reason to become a long-term resident of the "house of pain."

Tools to exit your "house of pain," and help you go from being the victim of your story to becoming the hero of your story:

- List and count all of your blessings and abilities, rather than listing all of your problems. Be thankful for what you do have. Gratitude has the positive effect of helping to lighten the load and blunting the sharpness of emotional pain.

- Refuse to say, "Poor me." Substitute "Poor me" with "There are those who have it worse than me and I choose to appreciate what I am fortunate to have and to move on."

- View the pain you have endured as a learning and character-building experience.

- Recall your past successes and relive them in your mind. The more you relive and think about them, the more you will feel encouraged and inspired to move forward and succeed.

- The very moment you feel self-pity coming on, swiftly stop it in its tracks by doing something nice for someone or tell the self-pity to "go and sit silently in the corner."

- Forgive anyone who might have hurt you, and—most of all—forgive yourself for carrying the burden of the pain for the time that you did.

Pack your bags, dash out the door—
there's a brighter life out there in store.

Chapter 42

Break Free, Leave the Past Behind

"I demolish my bridges behind me—then there is no choice but forward."
                                                        Fridtjof Nansen

Living in the past is like living in a cage, bound by your own self-made chains, stuck and unable to move forward.

Do not allow the past to define what you can do now, nor who you can become. This is now your chance to transform your past life experiences into wisdom.

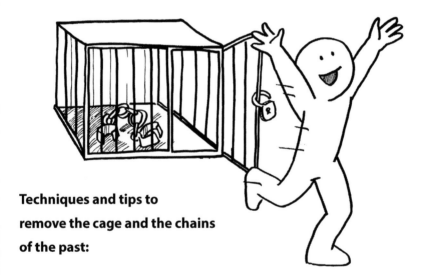

Techniques and tips to remove the cage and the chains of the past:

To begin with, it is helpful to accept the fact that anything which does not exist cannot be fixed. The Past does not exist, and therefore it too cannot be fixed. That being said, it's time to let the past go, to take a deep invigorating breath and only focus on The Right Now.

Read-to-be-Freed Technique

Read the real-life stories of the many men and women who overcame adversities and rebounded from their own low points. You don't have to just wonder how they succeeded, their strategies and experiences will inspire you and give you guidance.

Release Regrets and Negative Thoughts from the Past Technique

Read options 1 and 2, and choose which suits you best.

1. Close your eyes and visualize or imagine the regrets and negative thoughts from your past crumbling and turning to tiny particles of dust and leaving your body by whichever way you choose; maybe through the pores in your skin. Now sense or imagine a powerful wind lifting the dust particles and carrying them past the ends of the earth until they have all gone forever. Slowly open your eyes, stretch your arms feeling a sense of freedom.

2. Close your eyes and visualize or imagine jackhammers crumbling the regrets and negative thoughts into tiny pieces. Pour the tiny pieces into a jar and seal it closed. Place the jar in the basket of a nearby hot air balloon. Visualize the balloon rising higher and higher. As it approaches the sun, visualize the balloon, the basket, the jar and its contents all going up in flames and disintegrating into microscopic particles which disappear forever. Slowly open your eyes, stretch your arms, feeling a sense of freedom. If the jackhammers did not suit you, then imagine simply placing your regrets and negative thoughts in a container of your choice, closing it and dropping it into the balloon's basket just before its lift-off.

You can create any scenario that will work best for you. Practice these techniques several times.

• Make a list of all the things you are good at. Read this list at least twice a day. Repetition leads to reinforcement!

• To launch your new start, write down a list of all the things you would like to do, and then choose the one you would most like to start with. Focus only on the starting component of the project. When that is done, move swiftly to complete your project.

• If negative thoughts from the past arise, temporarily move to another chair or location. If there is a radio nearby, turn it on or create some other mental diversion.

From Stuck In The Past To Unstuck Visualization Technique

First read the following 5 steps and then commence:

1. Close your eyes and visualize or imagine yourself stuck.

2. Let that stuck image of yourself move away from you. The further away it moves, the duller, smaller and fuzzier it becomes.

3. With your eyes still closed, visualize or imagine a bright and colorful picture of yourself, no longer stuck in the past, and now looking vibrant and free.

4. Intensify the picture; make it even brighter and more colorful. Feel the feeling of freedom and renewal throughout your body, all the way from the top of your head to the tips of your fingers, and all the way down to the tips of your toes. Intensify the feeling.

5. Open your eyes, and for about a second each look up, look down, look left, and then right. This is what's known as the break state and is an integral part of the process.

Repeat this sequence 10 times, twice a day, for about 3 weeks.

Each time you practice this Stuck In The Past to Unstuck Technique, allow your new, bright, and liberated image of yourself to dominate and outshine the dull, smaller, fuzzier image of your past.

There is a road you are free to take:
from stuck in the past, shackled in your cell,
to unstuck at last and doing well.

Chapter 43

Start Feeling Good Enough

"What you get by achieving your goals is not as important as what you become by achieving your goals."

Henry David Thoreau

There are times in your life when you may feel that you are not good enough. You are not alone. At some time or another almost every person on the planet has these feelings. These feelings are not productive, but fortunately, with due effort, you can overcome them and have a better life.

Techniques and suggestions to help you start feeling good enough:

- Whenever you feel that someone else is superior to you, it is wise to acknowledge that there are people more talented than you, richer than you, and smarter than you. This will always be true. But there are also people who are not as talented as you, poorer than you, and not as smart as you. Let this knowledge and understanding help you feel comfortable with where you are at this particular moment in your life.

- Whatever your makeup, each of us is a unique person with a positive and contributing role to play. Don't compare yourself to the rich and the beautiful, the influential and the famous who appear in every form of media 24/7. Don't think less of yourself because these people exist. You have no idea what real challenges and limitations some of them and their family members might be facing. If you knew the truth of their lives, you may not want to trade places with them.

• Don't compare yourself to other people. Rather compare yourself to how you were yesterday and how you are today. Comparison is the thief of joy.

• Don't waste time watching other people climbing their ladders. Climb your own ladders, one determined step at a time! Each step up will increase your feeling of being good enough.

BECOMING
GOOD ENOUGH

• Notice how successful people have reached their goals. Learn from them. Follow what they did to succeed, and if needed, make the necessary adjustments to reach your own goals.

• Recall a time when you were successful. Close your eyes and relive that event. Now, throughout your body, feel the good feelings associated with that success. Let those feelings and memories motivate and inspire you to succeed again. Because you succeeded before, you CAN succeed again!

• Think of someone, alive or not, who loves or admires you. Write down the good qualities that you know that person sees in you. Make a point of reading this list often. The more you read it, the more you will be reminded of all your good qualities, and the more these qualities will be imprinted into your subconscious mind. Repeatedly imprinting positive facts and thoughts into the subconscious mind has the effect of increasing your self-esteem and your feelings of being good enough. Go to Chapter 4 – Thoughts and Feelings, to see how repetition increases this positive effect.

If someone ever said to you, things like: "You are not good enough" or "You will be just like your loser cousin," a very effective technique to help squash all that is to simply hear those words in a high-pitched or squeaky tone, as if they were being said or "squeaked" by a cartoon mouse. You will find this has the effect of minimizing those untrue words. In place of the mouse, you can use any voice or character that works effectively for you.

• A very powerful tool is to say these words out loud and with total conviction and meaning: **"I forgive myself for all the untrue stories I have been telling myself about myself."**

• While you are making progress on your path from "not feeling good enough" to "starting to feel good enough", don't despair or want to give up if you have some "not so good days." The path to success can have its hurdles to overcome, and besides, smooth seas don't make good sailors.

Feeling the start of feeling good enough is the start of the positive feeling of knowing you have a purpose and a place on the planet.

- **"Feeling good enough about yourself" can be given a tremendous boost by earning your own self-respect.** Begin earning your self-respect by selecting a relatively small project and working hard at it. As soon as the project is complete, pat yourself on the back, celebrate if you want, and move on to increasingly more challenging projects. If you fall, or something goes a little wrong, no worries, pick yourself up, make any necessary adjustments and continue on.

- **Self-talk is the private conversations we have with ourselves.** The talk can be positive or negative. Saying comments like "great job, way to go," for even the smallest of achievements, either out loud or to yourself, informs your neural system, your subconscious and your inner-self that you are beginning to do well and are on the right track. Negative comments like "I have just messed up again," have the opposite effect—they wear you down. Instead, say "next time I aim to get it right."

• Take classes in computer skills or pottery or whatever else is appealing to you. As your skills increase so will your feeling of achievement and thoughts of being good enough. Volunteering serves a "double purpose." While being a great opportunity to assist others, it simultaneously elevates your self-worth and feelings of being good enough.

• Go to Chapter 45 - Boost Your Confidence. Read and practice the Circle of Excellence Technique found there.

• Our thoughts are often the culprits that make us feel not good enough. For help in dealing with self-limiting thoughts go to Chapter 40 - Throw Out Self-Doubts and Negative Thoughts.

• Be patient with yourself and when you make a mistake say, "It's OK."

• You don't have to actually feel good enough to be good enough. Often we have the skills to perform, but don't allow ourselves to do so.

• Look up the poem "Desiderata". Take special note of the lines that point out that it is best not to compare yourself to others, that you are not inferior, that you are deserving enough and that you have every right to be here. This poem is rich in wise words and suggestions. It is an excellent guide to good living.

Chapter 44

Better Perceptions—Better Life

"All our knowledge has its origin in our perceptions."

Leonardo da Vinci

It is important to know that how we perceive people and things is how we react to them.

Change your perception and you will react differently.

Here's a simple example to illustrate this point:
 If you were always taught, and consequently believe, that black dogs will harm you, you probably make every effort to avoid black dogs, no matter how inconvenient.

Later, when you become aware that there is no sense or truth to your belief that black dogs will cause you harm, you will have a change of outlook and become perfectly comfortable having them near you. What we learned growing up affects our perceptions throughout our lives. Fortunately, whatever negative stuff we learned can be unlearned by seeing it from a different and more positive point of view. It's as easy as that!

Here is another example of how differing perceptions affect our lives. Two people hike through a thickly-wooded forest. When they reach midway, a fierce storm begins. Within minutes, the howling winds snap twigs and branches off the trees sending them flying all over the forest.

To avoid being injured by the flying branches and falling trees, the two hikers run as fast as they can all the way to the edge of the forest.

When they emerge from the forest, they each express totally different experiences.

The smiling hiker viewed the event as a rare opportunity to witness up close the wild force of nature. In addition, he felt exhilarated and invigorated from having to push himself mentally and physically to escape from the forest. He had a great day. The scowling hiker, on the other hand, saw the experience as horrible and he complained non-stop about how exhausted he was. He had an awful day.

Conclusion: Each man had a totally different perception of the same set of circumstances, which resulted in the smiling hiker having a wonderful experience while the scowler had an awful time. When you change your perceptions and view unpleasant situations from more positive angles, life becomes brighter and more enjoyable.

Here is yet another example of how your perceptions have a powerful influence on your thoughts and decision-making. This is the representation of a photo that appears in a newspaper. What caption would you give to describe the photo? Is it "Thug beats innocent man with club?"

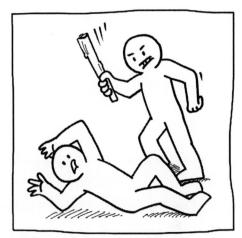

Now see the two figures from another view or perspective and what you have in front of you is a totally different picture. The caption could now quite easily read "Passerby overpowers mugger and confiscates his club." Perceptions! Perceptions! Perceptions!

Become Positively Perceptive Technique:
How much more happy and relaxed we would be if we observed everything with a positive view. If at first you struggle to have a positive view, do the following:

1. View a particular situation from a negative perspective.
2. Next, examine the situation from a positive perspective.
3. Spend a few minutes pondering some of the positive aspects that come up. Just the recognition and appreciation of one or two of the positive aspects will start the habit of seeing things from a positive point of view.

Chapter 45

Boost Your Confidence

"Confidence is that feeling by which the mind embarks on great and honorable courses with a sure belief and trust in itself."

Cicero

Confidence is a game-changer and fortunately, with some effort, it can be developed and enhanced. An attitude of confidence allows you to have a positive view of yourself and your situation. It enhances your ability to take on assignments, to step out of your comfort zone and to take risks knowing that if you fail you will be able to get up and start again.

Please note that having a low level of confidence not always implies that you do not have the know-how or skills to succeed. They are two separate items.

Techniques and tips to increase confidence:
• During your formative years, you may have been tainted by negative surroundings and by people who made you feel inadequate and unworthy. Now that you have matured, it is wise to look back and discover that it was not you who caused those feelings of inadequacy and lowered confidence. It usually was the unwarranted comments from a family member or a person of authority, like a school teacher, that caused this negativity to become imprinted into your subconscious mind. These imprints become the false truths and the lies about yourself that go on to shape your future thoughts and actions. Since "hurt people, hurt people," it is very important to note

that the person who abused or hurt you in your past, or is hurting you today, was probably hurt at some time in his life, and he took, or is currently taking, his misfortune out on you. For more help with this situation, see Chapter 16 – The Power and Benefits of Forgiving, and Chapter 43 – Start Feeling Good Enough.

• Self-assured, confident people recognize themselves as being individuals with a positive role to play. Confident people do not worry about disapproval or negative comments from others. They believe that it is not essential to conform to what everybody else is saying or doing in order to be accepted.

• Do not be concerned about meeting the expectations of family and society. You do not have to prove anything to anybody.

• Do not set unrealistic and unattainable goals that might set you up for failure. Failing is okay, but failing because the goals were unreachable from the start could unnecessarily decrease your level of confidence.

• Be realistic and acknowledge that you cannot always be the best at everything you do.

• Boost your confidence by doing something that you are afraid of. Be sensible in what you choose to do.

• Take care of your appearance. Being well groomed is a definite confidence booster. Besides, you never know who you will run into!

Circle Of Excellence Technique

This technique enables you to rapidly produce a more confident state of mind. It will help to increase your performance for a particular occasion, like making a presentation. It is also helpful when you need to go on a job interview, participate in a sporting or social event and any other occasion that can be enhanced with a feeling of confidence. The Circle of Excellence Technique, was developed by Dr. J. Grinder and Dr. J. DeLosier. It works by rapidly recalling and infusing yourself with the positive feelings and resources you experienced during a previous successful event or circumstance.

1. Visualize or imagine a circle on the floor about two feet in front of you and about three feet in diameter. When first practicing, you can use string or chalk to mark the circle.

2. Select an upcoming challenging situation — an interview, a presentation, a social event, etc.

3. Recall a successful experience you once had. (It can be unrelated to the current challenging situation you face.)

4. Step into the circle and relive the good feelings of that past experience.

Visualize that successful scene and feel the good feelings you felt back then. Hear any associated sounds you heard back then.

5. Amplify step 4. Make the recollections of the past event even more vivid and feel within you the associated increase in positive energy. Apply an anchor as you recall and sense the resources, memories and positive energy you had back then. (See notes below for anchor description.)

6. Visualize yourself at the future event, equipped with all of your positive resources, filled with confidence and feelings of success.

Practice this technique and notice your confidence rising. At the actual event, "step" into your imagined circle, apply your anchor, and feel your positive recollections and resources filling you and readying you for success.

Notes:

• An anchor is used to help trigger your instant recall of the beneficial resources, good thoughts, positive feelings and sounds associated with a time or event from the past.. Examples of an anchor: connecting your thumb and index finger, making a fist or touching your wrist. You may choose any other anchor that works best for you.

• My clients have increased their levels of confidence by "painting" the circle a color that represents confidence to them. You can choose to experience the "confidence color" entering your body through the soles of your feet and filling your entire mind and body with confidence.

• In addition to the Circle of Excellence you can use "The 'Blank' of Excellence" which can be adapted to any specific situation, for example, the chair you sit on at a business or social meeting can be your "Chair of Excellence. "The podium from where you speak can be your "Podium of Excellence." The keyboard on which you type article or letters can be your "Keyboard of Excellence." Select any situation that will work for you.

• For another effective confidence gaining technique, go to the "Be The Change Technique" found in Chapter 35 - Changing Habits and Behaviors.

Chapter 46

Minimize That Annoying Person

"Do not let the behavior of others destroy your inner peace."

Dalai Lama

Most of us, at one time or another, come across a person who can be downright annoying.

You appreciate and enjoy his good qualities, but things about him drive you nuts. Maybe he can easily become argumentative or will never admit he's wrong. Maybe it's an over-bearing family member who just does not know when enough is enough. In my practice, using the following technique to minimize or eliminate the impact of an annoying person has had successful results.

Clown Technique

1. Visualize painting a clown's face on the annoying person. Next, place a neon-colored wig on his head. If you want, you can place a clown's hat on top of the wig.

You might also want to see him dressed up as a clown, wearing funny clown shoes.

2. Once you have done that, hear everything coming out of his mouth as squeaks, or whatever sounds are silly and comical to you.

3. Having completed step 2, on a scale of 1-10, (where 10 is extremely annoying), at what level of annoyance is

The Clown Technique

that person to you right now? You will find that the more humorous the sounds coming out of the clown's mouth, and the more comical he looks, the less annoying or threatening he becomes. You are not limited to a clown's face; use any face or character that is comical to you.

As a bonus, those annoying people might stop their irritating behavior when they realize they are not being heard the way they want to be heard.

Chapter 47

Reading Other People's Minds

"If you wish to know the mind of man, listen to his words."

Chinese proverb

Have you ever walked into a room full of people and felt really uncomfortable because you "knew" that some of those people were thinking unfavorable things about you?

Or, have you ever had a disagreement in a relationship and you could tell what was going on in the other person's mind? You knew what he was thinking, and knowing his thoughts caused you to become uncomfortable, anxious, fearful, or angry.

Whenever a client informs me that he knows what another person is thinking, we have the following conversation:

Me: So you have just told me that you know what's going on in that other person's mind. Is that correct?

Client: That's correct. I read his mind.

Me: Oh, so you read his mind?

Client: Yes, I read his mind.

Me: Okay, next time there is a street fair in your area, I would like you to call the organizers and book a 10-foot by 10-foot booth for yourself. Next, I want you to make a huge banner, that says "Mind

Reader," which you will display prominently in your booth. Now, close your eyes and imagine yourself sitting in your booth and reading the minds of all the people who are waiting patiently in a long line and are happy to pay $20 for you to read their minds. Now, see that pile of $20 bills becoming larger and larger every time you read another mind. Okay, so will you call the organizers today to book your Mind Reader's booth for the next street fair?

Client: No.

Me: Why not?

Client: Because I am not a mind reader.

We often mistakenly think that we can read other people's minds and in so doing, we make unnecessary problems for ourselves. Quit being a mind reader, you are engaging in the impossible!

Just as we cannot read another person's mind, no one can read our mind. If you want someone to know what is on your mind, you have to tell the person.

Chapter 48

Make Socializing Easier

"I am not afraid of storms, for I am learning how to sail my ship."
                                                    Louisa May Alcott

Humans have a need to meet with other humans to talk and interact. You don't have to be the most outgoing, the loudest or the most bubbly to be a successful socializer; and if you are not a naturally social person, you can learn.

Ways to make your socializing easier:

- If you are uneasy about going to an event, give yourself a reason to go. Adopt the mindset that you might meet interesting people, or you might come across business networking possibilities.

- Be curious about people, it makes them feel worthwhile and interesting and will often lead to good conversation.

- There are many ways of starting a conversation with another person. Here are some ice breakers and conversation starters. Compliment the person on an item of their clothing or a piece of jewelry. Ask what kind of work she does, ask if she lives in the neighborhood; if she is from out of town, ask her about her town. Ask if he is planning a vacation any time, if not, ask where he would like to go. Ask what kind of movies or books she enjoys, and which she would recommend. Ask how he knows the host. Suggest a way you might be able to help him gain customers or increase business. Inquire which team he supports and how they're doing this season. Always bear in mind that people tend to enjoy talking about themselves and sharing their likes and dislikes, so it's a good strategy to get someone talking by asking simple basic questions about everyday life.

- Feel good about how you look. This increases your self-confidence and makes you more attractive to others.

- Be cheerful and positive. People would rather chat to someone with a cheery disposition than someone with a dark cloud hanging over their head.

- Keep up with local and world news. Asking people their opinion about current events is a convenient conversation opener.

- The feeling of self-consciousness can be reduced by holding a drink in your hand. Just the small effort required to hold the glass is enough to divert and decrease some of your nervous energy.

- If at an event you feel uncomfortable because you sense that people are directing their thoughts and stares at you, I invite you to overcome this feeling by using what I call the "too-busy tool." It goes like this: "Don't worry about what you think other people are thinking about you, because they are too busy thinking about what others are thinking about them."

- If you are convinced that you can read people's minds and you are sure that they are thinking negative thoughts about you and, in the process, hurting your socializing experience, then I suggest that you go to Chapter 47 - Reading Other People's Minds.

- There are social sites on the internet that give notice of events and gatherings where like-minded people can participate in activities and meet new people. Visit the various groups until you find those that suit you best.

- If you feel someone is ignoring you, it could easily be that the person is momentarily occupied by some personal or unrelated issue. Don't take it personally. Instead, chat with someone else. Besides, everyone is not expected to get along with everyone.

- Be an attentive listener. This offers you the opportunity to pick up and continue the conversation thread, adding whatever you think is relevant.

- If your confidence needs a boost, practice the Circle of Excellence technique found in Chapter 45 - Boost Your Confidence.

Help With Socializing Shyness Technique

If shyness is in the way of your socializing, adopt this technique:

1. Before going to the event, find a quiet spot where you can lie down or sit comfortably.

2. Close your eyes and for a few minutes focus on your breathing.

3. Now visualize or imagine yourself at the event looking and feeling calm and relaxed. See yourself chatting with people, then walking across and chatting to someone else.

4. Open your eyes and stretch. Go off to the event and take with you the positive visuals you visualized and the positive feelings you felt.

Two more facts about socializing:

- Don't wait for people to initiate a conversation with you; you'll meet new people faster by opening conversations with them!

- Whenever you meet a stranger, remember that "a stranger is just a friend you do not know." If you stop and think back, many of your friends were once strangers.

Chapter 49

Stepping Out Of A Rut

"The first step towards getting somewhere is to decide that you are not going to stay the way you are."   *J.P. Morgan*

There are times when we get into a rut. Being stuck in a rut causes feelings of lethargy and boredom. During those times, it seems like life is just endless days of nothing with little to get excited about.

When you start doing things differently and engage in activities that you have never done before, the chances are strong that you will begin to feel things changing for the better.

Ways to get out of the rut:

- Take a different way home from work. When traveling along a different or less familiar route, the mind tends to operate less on "autopilot," causing you to be more conscious and aware of the new surrounding area and to also gain new perspectives.

- Stop in a neighborhood you have rarely or never visited. Take a walk along its streets and pathways, explore the stores and galleries.

Experiencing unfamiliar or different locations can prompt you to have fresh vistas and new ideas, which, in turn, could evolve into motivating opportunities and positive and brighter situations.

- **If words similar to "I'm stuck" are in your mind, replace them with words like "I'm figuring out new directions."** By doing so, your subconscious mind becomes activated into helping you lift yourself out of your rut. I cannot overstate enough the importance of firing up your subconscious mind.

- **Identify, write down and take action.** Briefly write down why you feel you are in a rut. Writing down the reasons might seem an unnecessary drag, but it is useful to better define your thoughts. In addition, when you actually see the reasons clearly written out in front of you, they become more real and, depending on your intentions, they become more actionable. Recognizing the reasons why you got into the rut is a vitally important step. Perhaps a situation at work is holding you back from achieving your potential or perhaps you no longer find your job fulfilling. Maybe it's time to end a relationship. Perhaps the part of town you are living in is not as appealing as it used to be. Whatever the reasons, once you identify them, do the next big thing—take immediate action. Making the change or changes might be tough, but if you genuinely want the changes and view the effort as being well worth it, then your motivation and sense of purpose will increase accordingly. When there is purpose, it is somehow much easier to make the effort. Goodbye rut!

- Make a list of things you have always wanted to do. It may be a hobby, a craft, a sport, a cultural activity. Choose one and do it. You don't have to be an expert at any of them. A most beneficial by-product of taking part in activities or hobbies, is that when you are actively absorbed in them, any negative thoughts that might come into your mind tend to be crowded out or pushed aside.

- Be bold—enjoy the liberating spirit of adventure by doing something that in the past would have seemed beyond you.

- Use the internet to find social groups. You'll be surprised; there are a wide range of groups that cater to a broad spectrum of interests. Select a group that interests you and check it out. Aside from participating in activities, this is an opportunity to meet new people. You never know, one of those people might inspire you to lift yourself out of your rut and go from stuck to unstuck.

- Keep going—even small steps will get the ball rolling.

Tired of being in the same old harbor?

Raise your anchor and sail to another.

Chapter 50

Overcoming Rejection

"Beware of allowing a tactless word, a rebuttal, a rejection to obliterate the whole sky."   *Confucius*

No matter who you are, rejection in one form or another will happen now and then.

Rejection can happen in almost any area and in any way. For example, you may experience rejection in relationships, in social groups, or in competitive endeavors. However, by working to avoid rejection altogether, you will limit the possibilities life offers.

Rejection: Reasons and Remedies

- Rejection is never pleasant, but when you acknowledge that the rejector's decision could have been influenced by factors beyond your control, or even beyond the rejector's control, then your perceptions change and the sting subsides.

- You didn't get the job. Perhaps the person who conducted your job interview was having an overbearing personal problem that day and didn't pay you the attention you deserved. Maybe the company made sudden changes to the skill set originally required. Again, accepting that there could be a host of different reasons, none of which have anything personally to do with you, reduces the upset.

- Maybe the person you would like to have a relationship with is not as ready as you are. This person might still be dealing with his or her own issues and reservations, which perhaps are the result of a past relationship gone wrong.

- Since each one of us is unique, with our own likes, dislikes and values, this is reason enough to accept that not everyone is destined to get along.

- Remember that an opinion is only an opinion, and therefore being rejected may not necessarily be the truth about your ability, character, or personality. If a person has a negative opinion of you, it might be because her perspectives and values are flawed or because her perspectives and values are not in sync with your own.

- The product you submitted to a craft show was turned down. This could have happened not because your entry was not good enough, but because the organizers had decided at the last moment to place more emphasis on exhibiting other kinds of crafts.

- When you feel hurt by rejection, do not to dwell on it. Rather, think of those who love and admire you, or of the times when you were successful.

- An important aspect of the Rejection Remedies is for you to accept your contribution to any rejection that might have occurred. Be totally honest with yourself. Perhaps, in the case of an interview, you were not adequately prepared or suitably dressed. If you recognize and acknowledge that all or part of your rejection was caused by something you did, then be fair to yourself and make the appropriate changes so this situation doesn't reoccur.

Chapter 51

Inner Conflicts

"Two souls, alas, are housed within my breast, and each will wrestle for the mastery there."   *Johann W. von Goethe*

At times, most of us have a conflict going on within us. Fortunately, when faced with an inner conflict, we usually have the freedom to choose how to resolve it. Do we, for example, take the more difficult road which we know will offer the long-term best solution for us and those around us, or do we do take the easier path which probably has questionable consequences?

Do we choose to make a point of having good thoughts, or do we allow ourselves to be overcome with negative thoughts? Do we consciously care about other people, or do we pay little attention to anyone beyond ourselves? Do we give in to temptation or do we hold ourselves back?

The following wisdom, borrowed from Native American teachings, clearly illustrates the "conflict that is within us" situation and indicates that we have a choice in its resolution.

One evening, an elderly warrior told his grandson about a battle that goes on inside all people.

He said, "The battle is between the two wolves inside of us. One wolf is bad. It is anger, envy, jealousy, sorrow, regret, greed, arrogance, self-pity, guilt, resentment, lies, false pride, superiority and ego. The other wolf is good. It is joy, peace, love, optimism, serenity, humility, kindness, benevolence, empathy, generosity, truth and compassion." The grandson thought about it for a minute and then asked his grandfather:

"Grandfather, which wolf wins the battle?"
The wise old warrior replied: "The one that you feed."

Which wolf are you feeding the most? Would you prefer to feed the other?

Chapter 52

Feel Comfortable Starting Over

"Every morning we are born again. What we do today is what matters most."
                                                            Buddha

If you are feeling disheartened because things are not working out for you and your future is looking bleak, remember that it's not over and you can move on. It is helpful to view this time as a bend in the road not the end of the road.

Even if everything is wrong in your life today, it doesn't have to continue that way. The best way to start over is to waste no time and get moving again. Once you have made the decision to start over, keep looking ahead and never look back.

Abraham Lincoln's story is a shining example of "It's not over." Read the following list of events in his life and you might agree that it's never over.

- 1831 – Lost his job
- 1832 – Defeated in run for Illinois State Legislature
- 1833 – Failed in business
- 1834 – Elected to Illinois State Legislature (success)
- 1836 – Had nervous breakdown
- 1838 – Defeated in run for Illinois House Speaker
- 1843 – Defeated in run for nomination for U.S. Congress
- 1846 – Elected to Congress (success)
- 1848 – Lost renomination
- 1849 – Rejected for land officer position

- 1854 – Defeated in run for U.S. Senate
- 1856 – Defeated in run for Vice President.
- 1858 – Again defeated in run for U.S. Senate
- 1860 – Elected President (success)

With all of that, Lincoln went on to become one of America's finest and most memorable of presidents!

When things go wrong and all seems lost, take a hard look at all of the positive possibilities out there. **In golfing terms, don't spend time gazing at the sand traps and waterholes — rather visualize the ball flying on a new path on its way toward the cup.** You will make it easier on yourself when you view starting over not as a difficulty but rather as an opportunity to focus on your strengths and abilities to successfully build up again.

Starting over is also an opportunity to launch into something completely new — a chance to reinvent yourself. Reinvention performed with passion and determination is an exhilarating and rewarding experience. By its very nature starting over opens up new worlds of possibilities—view it as a whole new adventure. See page 183 on Opportunitrees.

Your story is not over. keep turning your pages

Chapter 53

Advice to Caregivers

"You give but little when you give of your possessions. It is when you give of yourself that you truly give."

Kahlil Gibran

Caregivers may find their energy becoming depleted by the negative energy they feel from some of those in their care. There are ways to prevent this energy depletion from happening.

• If the person in your care becomes angry or yells at you, it is best to avoid having a knee-jerk reaction and yelling back. Unless there is an urgent rush to respond, take a calm approach and thoughtfully consider your response. Reply in your normal speaking voice.

• Bear in mind that the patient might be feeling frustrated or angry about his limitations and pain and that yelling or complaining to another human is how he is giving vent to his feelings. For this reason, there is no need to take the outbursts and complaints personally. Doing so will wear you down and could even cause you to feel resentful.

• To ensure that you can continue to be an able caregiver, exercise sufficiently, get fresh air, eat healthy, set aside time for yourself, take up an interest and practice mindfulness. See Chapter 57 – Mindful Methods in Minutes, and the other chapters that specifically address these points.

• Join a caregivers support group. Besides learning new ways to deal with your patient, this will also be an opportunity for you to socialize.

Caregiver's Ring of Protective Flames Technique
To keep your energy from depleting, or otherwise being negatively impacted by those in your care, visualize or imagine yourself surrounded by a low ring of special room temperature Caregiver Protective Flames. The flames can be any color you choose. These are not harmful flames, but flames that only cause the destruction and disintegration of all the negative energy that might be given out by whomever is in your care.

Chapter 54

Reducing Physical Pain

"The mind has great influence over the body, and maladies often have their origin there."
Jean Moliere

The mind is a powerful healing tool and can play a role in making the pain wane. Using our imagination, we can visualize almost anything. As was discussed earlier in this book, guided imagery and visualization are age-old therapeutic techniques. Both are being used more frequently in Western medicine. By creating appropriate images in the mind, a person can reduce pain and its associated symptoms.

The following two techniques can have successful outcomes in the elimination or reduction of pain.

Color Replacement Technique

1. When you feel a pain, close your eyes and give it a color that best describes the painful feeling. For the sake of illustration, let's describe the pain as red.

2. Then think of a color that is most pleasant and healing to you. In this example, let's use pale green.

3. With your eyes still closed, focus on the red in the painful area and imagine the red beginning to move out of your body and into the air and evaporating away.

4. As the red moves out of the painful area, visualize or imagine it being replaced by the pleasant, gentle and healing pale green. The colors can be in liquid or vapor form, or in any other form that works best for you.

Spin Technique

1. Close your eyes and focus on the pain.

2. Imagine that the pain could spin in a clockwise or counter-clockwise direction.

Reverse the spin!

3. Rapidly establish the direction in which your pain is spinning. Then, to reduce the pain, immediately visualize or imagine the pain spinning in the opposite direction and, if you wish, give it a color you like..

These techniques might take some practice, so be a little patient.

Caution: Before using these techniques, I recommend that you check with your medical doctor to establish that there is no underlying cause of your pain that requires attention.

Chapter 55

Presurgery Preparation

"The treatment is really a cooperative of a trinity--the patient, the doctor and the inner doctor." *Ralph Bircher*

The calmer you are in mind and body, the more successful your surgery is likely to be. Guided imagery, visualizing and relaxation techniques can help to decrease anxiety and pain, strengthen the immune system and accelerate the body's healing process.

Techniques and suggestions for presurgery preparation:

• Feel comfortable with your doctor or surgeon.

• Ask questions. Having the answers and increasing your knowledge decreases anxiety and fears.

• Be aware that you are not alone, and that in almost all cases, many other people have undergone similar surgery. Remind yourself that your surgical team is well practiced and skilled at the procedure.

• Close your eyes and feel the love, warmth and support of all your well-wishers and those who will take care of you.

• Do the 18-second relaxing technique found in Chapter 7 – Quick and Easy Relaxation Techniques, several times a day. Do the muscle relaxing technique found in Chapter 8 – Progressive Muscle Relaxer, but do not apply this technique to that part of your body which is unhealthy or going to be operated upon.

• Visualize yourself after your surgery enjoying life to the fullest and best of your ability.

• A skilled certified hypnotherapist would be able to rapidly help you decrease your presurgery anxiety. Presurgery anxiety is linked to greater pain, increased need for painkillers and longer hospital stays. Your hospital might be offering hypnosis services. Therapeutic hypnosis is not to be confused with stage hypnosis, which is purely for entertainment. Furthermore, hypnosis is not mind control as it is often incorrectly depicted by the movie and television industry.

Chapter 56

Accelerate Your Postsurgery Healing

"If you only use a small portion of your mind, you will be amazed at how much you can achieve." *Thomas Alva Edison*

Be proactive in your recovery. Your mind has the potential to be a powerful healing tool.

An increasing number of major hospitals are acknowledging and using the power of the mind to hasten the healing process. You will be amazed at the beneficial roles your mind and the mind-body connection can play in accelerating both physical and emotional healing.

(To make this chapter even more meaningful for you, first read Chapter 2 – The Mind-Body Connection and Chapter 3 – Visualization and Guided Imagery.)

With your direction, your mind, together with your imagination, can accelerate post-surgery healing as well as the healing of many of the injuries you might sustain throughout life.

There are no hard and fast rules or directions on how to direct your mind to accelerate healing. Using the following suggestions, each person can direct and customize their own accelerated healing techniques.

Accelerated Healing Visualization Techniques:

• Create your own accelerated healing movies; you might find that you have fun doing this. Incidentally, fun and humor can contribute to faster healing by decreasing the body's stress levels. Be as creative as you wish. For example, you may wish to add sound and any other special effects to enhance the making of your Accelerated Healing Visualization movie.

Examples of healing visualizations:

• Relax, close your eyes, and imagine skilled miniature medical personnel busy working away within your wound area accelerating the healing process as they do.

• Visualize or imagine miniature submarines sailing effortlessly through your blood vessels toward the wound or surgery area where they drop off their cargoes of healing lotions. The submarines or boats can also deliver "get-well soon" cards from yourself to the wound area.

• Select a color that represents healing to you. Now, imagine that healing color, which may be in liquid or mist form, spreading itself in and around the wound area.

• Close your eyes, take a deep breath, exhale slowly and relax. Now, imagine being surrounded by healing white light, or a healing light color of your preference. Sense the healing light gently entering your body. Visualize or imagine it making its way to the wound area. Once it has arrived there, sense it focusing its healing light on the wound.

• You can further aid your body's healing by remaining calm and rested. Please note that there are calming and relaxing techniques for your use throughout this book.

Helping Healing…Harnessing The Power Of Your Mind

Chapter 57

Mindful Methods in Minutes

"Remember then: there is only one time that is important—
Now! It is the most important time because it is the only time
when we have any power."   Leo Tolstoy

Although some of the tools and techniques found in previous chapters are designed to deal with specific issues, they too will also enhance overall mindfulness. **But because mindfulness is so beneficial and so lifestyle-changing, it definitely warrants a chapter of its own!**

Mindfulness, which is closely related to "living in the now," has so many positive effects. In addition to playing a vital role in keeping one grounded and more aware of one's surroundings, mindfulness substantially increases feelings of well-being and reduces stress. This, in turn, strengthens the immune system to better ward off illness.

In life, mindfulness allows us the ability to more accurately assess situations, and to choose the more appropriate responses towards them. Additionally, mindfulness conditions us to become stronger, more steadfast and resilient, which in turn decreases the likelihood of our being stampeded into making hasty decisions or being negatively influenced by outside sources.

As explained in Chapter 4 – Thoughts and Feelings, our thoughts play a direct role in how we feel and act; instead of struggling with negative thoughts, mindfulness trains us to let them go and brings us back into the present moment, calming our minds and our bodies as it does.

Lengthy, mindful meditation sessions can be beneficial, however, they might not be convenient when you are pressed for time. Fortunately, the practice of mindfulness can be easily integrated into your daily routine by practicing the following quick yet effective methods. Let these mindfulness methods give you a beneficial break from the hustle and bustle of your day. They will help to increase the calm in your home and workplace and wherever you happen to be.

Hand-Wash Method

Hear the water rushing out of the faucet. Sense the temperature of the water against your skin. Be aware of the soapy, slippery feeling as your hands rub together. Notice the soap's aroma. While drying your hands be consciously aware of the texture of the towel against your skin.

Single-Raisin Method

1. Find a quiet place where you will not be disturbed for the next five minutes.

2. Place a raisin or other dried fruit in the palm of your hand. Sense its weight and look to see if it is casting a shadow.

3. Hold the raisin between your thumb and finger. Slowly move it around and become more aware of the feeling of its surface.

4. Closely observe its outer skin. Pay attention to the formation and architecture of the ridges and wrinkles. Notice the distinction between the brighter areas and the darker areas.

5. Become aware of any aroma the raisin might have.

6. Place the raisin in your mouth. Notice precisely how it feels on your tongue. Slowly roll it around.

7. Chew the raisin very slowly and deliberately. Pay close attention to the tastes it releases and to its changing texture. When the raisin is ground down and transformed into a fine paste, take notice of what your tongue does to prepare it for swallowing. Consciously swallow and imagine as best you can its path on the way down to your stomach.

Notes: You can also use the Single Raisin Method as

a guide for more conscious and deliberate detailed observance of the activities in your life. There might be a richness or a depth to activities that you previously passed by without ever noticing. In addition, use it as a guide to relive past pleasurable moments and events. Depending on what is being relived, this exercise can be calming or invigorating.

Meal-Prep Method

Turn what might be a chore into an opportunity to practice mindfulness. Food preparation, whether it be preparing a gourmet meal or making a sandwich, is an excellent opportunity for a session of mindfulness. Notice and feel the surfaces of the fruits and vegetables. Observe the colors and textures of the ingredients. Become aware of all the sounds associated with meal prepping: the chopping, the dicing, slicing, stirring, and boiling.

Notice and take in the distinct aroma offered up by the herbs and spices. As an added bonus, practicing this meal-prep mindfulness method is likely to reduce any fatigue you might feel after cooking a meal.

Flame-Focus Method

All you need is a quiet space, a table, a chair, a lighted candle, and three or four minutes. Focus on the flame. Notice how it changes shape. If thoughts enter your mind, refocus on the candle. With practice, you will focus on the flame undisturbed. (See note page 178.)

Notice-Nature Method

This method of practicing mindfulness involves selecting an element of nature and intently noticing its details. Fortunately, you don't have to hike through the wilds or walk along mountain trails to find wonders of nature upon which to focus your attention. There are many elements of nature in close proximity and readily available to you. Observe and appreciate the details of a single flower. Pause to watch raindrops hitting the ground. Sense the sun's warmth on your skin or the non-stop motion of waves as they continually roll to the shore. The list is endless—all you have to do is pause for a couple of minutes to focus on one particular element of nature. To enhance the experience, notice how this exercise is impacting on you while doing it.

Nearby-Object Method

Mindfulness can be practiced every day and everywhere. This particular method only requires two ingredients. The first is an object to hold or look at; it could be, for example, a cellphone, an ornament or a painting. The other ingredient is a few minutes of your focused attention. As you increase your focus on the object to the exclusion of everything else, become more and more aware of its shape, its lines, its texture and its colors. Experience, if you wish, a temporary merging of you and the object and feeling your ego becoming less and less.

Ground-Contact Method

When walking, either barefoot or in shoes, shift your focus to the soles of your feet. Become very aware of the feeling you feel in your soles as each foot makes contact with the ground. Further enhance this mindfulness contact experience by paying attention to the difference in the feeling in your soles when you walk onto another surface.

Notes: If distracting thoughts arise in your mind while you are practicing mindfulness, do not resist them or forcefully push them aside. This would give the thoughts undue prominence and distract your attention. One way is to simply greet each thought with a "hello thought" and let it go on its way while you continue with your mindfulness method.

Chapter 58

Happiness

"Happiness, not in another place but this place...not for another hour, but this hour."   *Walt Whitman*

Like most worthwhile desires in life, happiness will not be achieved simply by wishing and hoping. It takes effort, more effort and continuous effort. However, as you begin to recognize your level of happiness increasing the effort will seem well worth it. The suggestions set out below are intended to help increase your feelings of happiness:

- Be proactive in dismissing negative thoughts from the past. Do not worry about the future, rather, live in the now. These are all key components to attaining happiness. Specific ways to deal with the thoughts and worries that might limit your feelings of happiness are found in previous chapters of this book, including Chapter 38 – Worries, Fears And Catastrophic Thoughts and Chapter 40 – Throw Out Self-doubts and Negative Thoughts.

- Follow the view shared by many experienced and world-wise people who believe that happiness is not achieved by the conscious pursuit of happiness, but that it is generally the result or by-product of engaging in activities. These activities could be giving help to others, gardening, playing sports or a musical instrument, creating, learning, or whatever you wish. The list of activities to engage in is endless.

- Thinking optimistically also contributes to achieving happiness. A practical way of increasing your level of optimism is to challenge the validity of all your pessimistic thoughts the moment they come into your mind. See Chapter 43 – Start Feeling Good Enough. Also see Chapter 4 – Thoughts and Feelings on how the brain forms the neural pathways to help achieve a happier mindset.

- Accepting that you can be happy without acquiring everything you desire is one of the strongest foundations upon which the attainment of happiness is based.

- Learn to be satisfied with enough. Once your needs have been met; ask yourself if you need more.

- Free yourself from any hate and thoughts of vengeance that you have towards others. Forgive them, and then forgive yourself for having carried the burden of the pain – this will go a long way to increasing your happiness.

- It is wise to accept that life has its ups and downs—doing so reduces disappointments and frustrations. Since we cannot change the world to be the way each of us would like it to be, simply enjoying the little daily pleasures will reduce frustrations and increase your happiness.

- Don't be stiff and unbending like a rigid oak tree. When the winds blow hard, the oak tree is sometimes uprooted. Rather, be like the more flexible willow tree and bend with the wind so you don't get blown over or uprooted. After the storm has passed the willow is more likely to be the happy tree!

- Take good care of your physical and mental health.

- When you start feeling down, listen to upbeat, happy music; by helping to adjust your brain chemistry the music can rapidly help lift your mood.

- Don't take yourself too seriously or even your slightest mistake will make you miserable. Find the humor in life—laughter, including laughing at yourself, does wonders for wellbeing.

- Cut yourself and those around you some slack. It is unrealistic to expect perfect performances from yourself and others. It is difficult to experience happiness while being critical or down on yourself or anyone else. See Chapter 25 – You Don't Have to Be Perfect.

- Periodically stop what you are doing and take a minute to "smell the roses." Within your immediate surroundings, take notice of the good and pleasing elements you see. Appreciating and being thankful for the little things creates a feeling of happiness.

- Being out in nature is calming and likely to promote happiness and feelings of exhilaration.

- When others notice you doing what it takes to attain your happiness, you become an example for them to follow. By being the example, you are an **agent for positive change**; you are showing those people that it is possible for them to also attain and increase their own state of happiness.

- Help others to attain happiness, but don't be dependent on others to provide you with your happiness. Both in the short and long-term, it's best to be self-sufficient in the happiness department.

- **Above all, persevere. Never give up, and take the road that takes you where you choose to be. I wish you every success on your journey. Go for it and enjoy the resulting happiness.**

The Next Chapter
and Opportunitrees

I believe that a book devoted to self-improvement and achievement cannot, because of its very purpose, have a last or final chapter. This is because, for as long as we have breath, we have the ability to further expand our horizons, achieve more and increase our feelings of accomplishment and happiness.

Life goes on, and for as long as it does, there is no last chapter. What there are, however, are special trees, which are known as Opportunitrees.

Each Opportunitree is laden with possibilities, and one of those possibilities can become your next chapter.

Whenever you want to move on and expand your world, be on the lookout for an Opportunitree.

As soon as it comes into view, reach out and pick a possibility.
I wish you success and fulfillment in your next chapters.

Do your best, thrive and enjoy!

About the Author

In his life coaching practice, Alan Shein, works with a broad spectrum of clients, some of whom are referred by medical doctors. He helps his clients with a variety of issues including anxieties, stress, phobias, and sleeping difficulties. He assists clients with their limiting thoughts, emotions, and behaviors and in doing so helps them go from stuck to unstuck.

A key feature of Alan's practice is providing his clients with simple yet effective tools to take away with them. He has experience in and teaches people how to use the power of their minds.

In addition to helping and motivating business professionals, athletes, artists, and students to increase their performance levels, Alan also helps people with their current relationship issues and those whose relationships have ended.

Alan resides in San Diego, California. He sees clients in-office or long distance via Skype, and conducts group sessions on specific issues, including stress management, stress relief and mindfulness.

Interested readers can contact Alan directly through his website at BetterLifeLifeCoach.com

Suggested Reading

The Power of Self-confidence by Brian Tracy. John Wiley and Sons.

Forgiveness by Suzanne and Dr. Sydney B. Simon. Warner Books.

The Happiness Advantage by Shawn Achor. Crown Publishing.

Perfect Health: The Complete Mind/Body Guide by Deepak Chopra MD. Three Rivers Press.

Natural Relief for Anxiety by Edmund J. Bourne. New Harbinger Publications.

The Miracle of Mindfulness by Thich Nhat Hanh. Beacon Press.

Success Through a Positive Mental Attitude by Napoleon Hill. Pocket Books.

Solving the Procrastination Puzzle by Timothy A. Pychyl Ph.D. First Tarcher/Penguin Group.

The Emotional Life of Your Brain by Richard J. Davidson. Penguin Group.